The Believer's Secret of Intercession

The Believer's Secret of Intercession

Andrew Murray
C. H. Spurgeon

by Louis Gifford Parkhurst, Jr.

BETHANY HOUSE PUBLISHERS
MINNEAPOLIS, MINNESOTA 55438
A Division of Bethany Fellowship, Inc.

Published by Bethany House Publishers
A Division of Bethany Fellowship, Inc.
6820 Auto Club Road, Minneapolis, Minnesota 55438

Printed in the United States of America

Library of Congress Cataloging-in-Publication Data

Murray, Andrew, 1828–1917.
    The believer's secret of intercession.

    1. Prayer. I. Spurgeon, C. H. (Charles Haddon), 1834–1892.
II. Parkhurst, Louis Gifford, 1946-   . III. Title.
IV. Title: Intercession.
BV215.M867   1988   248.3'2   87-34145
ISBN 0-87123-992-2

Books by Andrew Murray

ANDREW MURRAY CHRISTIAN
MATURITY LIBRARY

The Believer's Absolute Surrender
The Believer's Call to Commitment
The Believer's Full Blessing of Pentecost
The Believer's New Covenant
The Believer's New Life
The Believer's Secret of a Perfect Heart
The Believer's Secret of Holiness
The Believer's Secret of Living Like Christ
The Believer's Secret of Obedience
The Believer's Secret of the Master's Indwelling
The Spirit of Christ

ANDREW MURRAY PRAYER LIBRARY

The Believer's Prayer Life
The Believer's School of Prayer
The Ministry of Intercessory Prayer
The Secret of Believing Prayer

ANDREW MURRAY DEVOTIONAL LIBRARY

The Believer's Daily Renewal
The Believer's Secret of Waiting on God
Day by Day with Andrew Murray

How to Raise Your Children for Christ

Authors

Andrew Murray was born in South Africa in 1828. After receiving his education in Scotland and Holland, he returned to South Africa and spent many years both as a pastor and missionary. He was a staunch advocate of biblical Christianity. He is best known for his many devotional books. He died in 1917.

Charles Haddon Spurgeon was born in England in 1834. Converted in 1850 in Artillery Street Primitive Methodist Church, he became a Baptist pastor in 1851. Called the "Prince of Preachers," he built the Metropolitan Tabernacle in London in 1859. Some say he experienced continuous revival throughout his ministry. In 38 years of ministry, he added over 14,000 members to his church, and preached enough sermons to fill 63 large volumes. He died in 1892.

L. G. Parkhurst, Jr., is a pastor of the First Christian Church of Rochester, Minnesota. He teaches ethics and logic at Minnesota Bible College, and is the editor and compiler of the Charles Finney "Principles Series" and other devotional books for Bethany House Publishers.

CONTENTS

Preface

The *Believer's Secret of Intercession* is the third book in a series where I have been combining Andrew Murray's "Secret" booklets with the writings of other well-known preachers or writers of devotional books. The first book, *The Believer's Secret of the Abiding Presence*, combined Murray's devotions with a book by Brother Lawrence. It emphasized being consciously present with the Lord Jesus Christ day by day and moment by moment, doing everything with the awareness of His abiding presence. The second book, *The Believer's Secret of Spiritual Power*, combined Murray's devotions with a book by Charles G. Finney. It emphasized the need for the Holy Spirit to empower us in our active, visible ministry for the Lord Jesus, showing our need to manifest the fruits and power of the Spirit. *The Believer's Secret of Intercession* has combined Murray's devotions with selections from some sermons by C. H. Spurgeon. It teaches us how to do that "hidden" labor for souls so blessings might fall upon the saints of God, and sinners might be converted in answer to fervent, prevailing prayer. How to offer effective intercessory prayer is an appropriate topic to follow these first two books, but this book can be read with great profit whether or not you have read the previous books in this series.

The name of C. H. Spurgeon still carries great weight

with devoted readers around the world. Even though Spurgeon died in 1892, his sermons were published in yearly volumes until 1917, when World War I brought a serious paper shortage in England. The reprinting of his sixty-three volumes of sermons has recently been completed by Pilgrim Publications of Pasadena, Texas.

Some believe that Spurgeon had a photographic memory and was what we would label today a "speed reader." He immersed himself in the writings of the Puritans and collected a large library of their works. A man of prayer and a gifted orator with immense intellectual capacity, Spurgeon was used by the Holy Spirit in amazing ways throughout his life. Bethany House Publishers has published a brief biography of this great man.

The Believer's Secret of Intercession combines Murray's classic booklet *The Secret of Intercession* with six of Spurgeon's sermons on this theme. Spurgeon's sermons on prayer could be edited into a few more books on different themes, so I have selected for use in this volume those specifically teaching about intercessory prayer. These are: "Intercessory Prayer," August 11, 1861; "Intercessory Prayer," May 5, 1872; "Intercession and Supplication," April 27, 1879; "Order and Argument in Prayer," July 15, 1866; "Praying in the Holy Ghost," November 4, 1866; "Prayer-Meetings," August 30, 1868. I could not use the entire sermons due to their length. Please use the prayers I have written at the end of each devotion to begin your own intercession, and not as a mere conclusion to your devotions.

Should you desire to continue your study of prayer with the use of daily devotional books, I have also compiled and edited *Principles of Prayer* and *Answers to Prayer* from the writings of Charles G. Finney, Bethany House Publishers; and *Pilgrim's Prayer Book* from the writings of John

Bunyan, Tyndale House Publishers. One of the most comprehensive books on prayer today is a collection of Charles G. Finney's sermons on prayer, *Principles of Devotion*, Bethany House Publishers.

Having compiled and edited *The Believer's Secret of Intercession*, I am now far more conscious of my need to spend more time in intercessory prayer. Persistent, fervent prayer is, perhaps, the greatest work that we can do by the grace of God. All Christians can perform this duty in the power of the Holy Spirit. I am convinced that in paradise God will be able to show us how everything achieved for Him was empowered by someone's prayers.

Spurgeon told his congregation: "No one can do me a truer kindness in this world than to pray for me." May we believe this of our friends and neighbors, our families and the dear saints we know! May we do them this "true kindness" and pray for them? May we also do this "true kindness" to the enemies of God and the Church so they might be saved and save others? When we come to believe that intercessory prayer is absolutely crucial because it can release the infinite power of Almighty God, then we will get on our knees and pray for the revival of the Church that Spurgeon and other great men of God in their time experienced as the result of united, prevailing prayer.

> With love in the Lamb,
> L. G. Parkhurst, Jr.

*P*ray one for another.

James 5:16

1

Intercession

What a mystery and glory there is in prayer! On the one hand, we see God in His holiness, love and power waiting and longing to bless us. On the other hand, by prayer we bring down from God the very life and love of heaven to dwell in our hearts.

Yet, there is a much greater glory in prayers of intercession. By intercession we boldly tell God what we desire for others. We seek to bring down blessings from God. We seek the power of eternal life with all its blessings upon one soul or perhaps upon hundreds and thousands.

Intercession! Do you believe that this can be the holiest exercise of your boldness as God's child? Do you practice intercession as the highest privilege and enjoyment connected with your conversation with God? Do you know the joy and the power of being used by God as an instrument for His great work of making people His habitation, of showing forth His glory?

The Church should count intercession as one of the chief means of grace. She ought to seek above everything to cultivate in God's children the power of an unceasing prayerfulness on behalf of the perishing world!

Believers, who have to some extent been brought into the secret of intercession, should feel the strength of united prayer. They need the assurance that God will certainly avenge His own elect who cry to Him day and night. Christians must stop looking for help in mere external union. They must be bound together by an unceasing devotion to Jesus Christ, so they can approach the throne of God in an unceasing supplication for the power of His Spirit. When the Church sees her true calling, then she will put on her beautiful garments and with new strength overcome the world.

The Practice of Intercession

Let me remind you that intercessory prayer has been practiced by all the best of God's saints. We may not find proof of answered prayer in every saint's biography, but without a doubt any person ever renowned for personal piety has been outstanding in his anxious desire for the good of others and diligent in his prayers for their benefit.

Look at Abraham, the father of the faithful. He earnestly pleaded for his son Ishmael: "O that Ishmael might live before thee!" On the plains of Mamre, he wrestled again and again for the city of Sodom, frequently reducing the number requested by God! How well he wrestled, and if we are sometimes tempted to wish he had not paused when he did, we must commend him for continuing so long for that depraved and doomed city.

Remember Moses, the most royal of men whether crowned or uncrowned. How often he interceded! How frequently do you meet with a record such as this: "Moses and Aaron fell on their faces before God"? Remember that cry of his on the top of the mount when, to his own personal disadvantage to intercede, he continued to pray even though God had said, "Let me alone, I will make of thee a great nation." He thrust himself in front of the axe of justice and cried, "Now, if thou wilt forgive their sin—; and if not [here he reached the very climax of agonizing earnestness], blot me, I pray thee, out of thy book." Never was there a mightier prophet than Moses and never one more intensely earnest in intercessory prayer.

Practice intercession for others with the fervency of Abraham and Moses, and you will save others in ways you could never have thought possible.

*D*ear Father, when I think about some of the great saints of old, such as Abraham and Moses, I feel so inadequate. They were so special, so courageous, so important, while I am so small by comparison. I pray that such examples will inspire me to intercede more fervently for others rather than bring discouragement. Grant me visible answers to specific prayers for others so I can be encouraged to continue interceding for other people and for the spread of your work on earth. In Jesus' name. Amen.

And Elisha prayed and said: Lord, open his eyes, that he may see. . . . And Elisha said, Lord, open the eyes of these men, that they may see.

2 Kings 6:17, 20

2

The Opening of the Eyes

*H*ow wonderfully the prayer of Elisha for his young servant was answered! The man saw the mountain full of the chariots of fire and horsemen around Elisha. The heavenly host had been sent by God to protect them.

Then Elisha prayed a second time. This time the Syrian army was smitten with blindness and led captive into the city of Samaria. There Elisha prayed for their eyes to be opened. And lo, they found themselves helpless prisoners in the hands of their enemy.

We wish to see these prayers in the spiritual sphere. First, we need to ask that our eyes may see the wonderful provision that God has made for His church in the baptism with the Holy Spirit. All the powers of the heavenly world are at our disposal in the service of the heavenly kingdom. Yet how little we live in the faith of that heavenly vision: the power of the Holy Spirit upon the disciples, with them and in them, for their own spiritual life and as their strength joyfully to witness for their Lord and His work!

Second, we need to pray that God may open the eyes of His children who do not see the power which the world and sin have upon His people. They are as yet unconscious of the feebleness that marks the Church, making it impotent to do the work of winning souls for Christ and building up believers for a life of holiness and fruitfulness. Let us pray especially that God may open all eyes to see what the great and fundamental need of the Church is: intercession to bring down His blessing that the power of the Holy Spirit may be known unceasingly in His divine efficacy and blessing.

The Practice of Intercession

There are many encouraging examples from the times of Christ and the apostles. Remember how Peter prayed on top of the house. Recall how Stephen prayed amid the falling stones. Or think, if you will, of Paul when he said that he never ceased to remember the saints in his prayers. He even stopped in the middle of writing a letter to say, "For which cause I bow my knee unto the God and Father of the Lord Jesus Christ." How many today pray for the Church and for this poor ungodly perishing world? A person is not a Christian if he does not pray for others.

We must be imitators of our blessed Lord Jesus Christ. On earth, He was preeminently the Intercessor. If you could have seen Him coming forth in the morning to preach the gospel and heal the sick, you might have seen how His garments were covered with the dew that had fallen upon Him as He had knelt all night in prayer to His Father. He could often truly say, "My head is filled with dew, and my locks with the drops of the night." See Him as He spent the whole night upon a lone mountainside agonizing for the souls of those He loved. His sorrowful lament was a flash of fire that always burned within His heart: "O Jerusalem, Jerusalem, thou that killest the prophets, and stonest them which are sent unto thee, how often would I have gathered thy children together, even as a hen gathereth her chickens under her wings, and ye would not!" The tears that fell from our Savior's eyes as He wept over Jerusalem dropped from a cloud that always rested on His soul, which was filled with a deep sympathetic compassion even for those who despised and rejected Him.

And now today, see Him with the eyes of faith as John saw in the Book of Revelation. He has put on His royal, priestly vesture, white as snow; and wearing a golden girdle, He stands amid the harps of angels and the songs of seraphs before His Father's throne as our great Intercessor still, for He ever lives to make intercession for us.

*D*ear Father, the sharp contrast between Elisha's visible success in prayer and the crucifixion of the Great Intercessor is overwhelming until I remember that by His death He won a greater spiritual battle over sin than Elisha's victory over the Syrian host. Help me to remember that Christ still lives to pray for others, and the Holy Spirit indwells me to inspire my prayers. Inspire me to keep on praying whether or not I see visible results today. For Jesus' sake, and the sake of His people. Amen.

The heaven, even the heavens, are the Lord's; but the earth hath he given to the children of men.

Psalm 115:16

3
Man's Place in God's Plan

God created heaven as a dwelling for himself: perfect, glorious and most holy. He gave the earth to people as their dwelling: everything very good at the beginning, with the need of being kept and cultivated. The work God did on earth, we are to continue and to perfect. Think of the iron and the coal hidden beneath the earth, of the steam hidden away in the water. God wanted us to discover and to use all of this. And what happened? We see a network of railways that span the continents and ships that cover the ocean. God created all to be used. He made the discovery and the use dependent upon our wisdom and diligence.

What the earth is today, with its cities and towns, with its cornfields and orchards, it owes to mankind. The work God began was to be carried out in fulfillment of His purpose by mankind. God calls us into a wonderful partnership with himself, to carry out the work of creation to its destined end.

This law holds equally good in the kingdom of grace. In this great redemption, God has revealed the power of the heavenly life and the spiritual blessings of which heaven is full. But He has entrusted to His people the work of making these blessings known.

What diligence the children of this world show in seeking the treasures that God has hidden in the earth for their use! Shall not the children of God be equally faithful in seeking the treasures hidden in heaven, to bring them down in blessing on the world? By the unceasing intercession of God's people, His kingdom will come and His will shall be done on earth as it is in heaven.

The Practice of Intercession

The piety of some people is comfortably confined within the limits of their own selfish interests. It is enough for them if *they* hear the Word of God, if *they* are saved, if *they* get to heaven. Ah, these miserable people will not get there! There would need to be another heaven for them, for the heaven of Christ is the heaven of the unselfish, the temple of the large-hearted, the bliss of loving hearts, the heaven of those who, like Christ, are willing to become poor that others may be rich.

I cannot believe, if I could ever believe, that the man whose prayers are selfish has the Spirit of Christ—it would be a libel upon the cross of Christ and a scandal upon the doctrines He taught. I commend intercessory prayer because it opens our hearts, enlarges our compassion, and constrains us to realize that we are not the center of the universe. Intercessory prayer teaches us that this wide world and this great universe were not made so we can be its petty lord, so everything should bend to our wills and all creatures bow at our feet.

It does us good to remember that the cross of Christ was not lifted for us alone, for its far-reaching arms were meant to shed blessings upon millions of the human race. Intercessory prayer can make the lean and hungry worshiper of self into a man more like the Son of Man.

The cloud hangs above you; it is yours to draw down its sacred showers of blessings by earnest prayers. God has put high up in the mountains of His promises springs of love; it is yours to bring down His blessings upon others by the divine channel of your intense intercessions. Intercede for others, lest God should say to you, because you have shut out your compassion for others, "You are not my child. You do not have my Spirit. You are not a partaker of my love. You shall not enter my rest." Let us be Christians in the fullest measure; let us have compassionate minds that can pray for others.

Dear heavenly Father, I am prone to pray for material blessings for others. I am inclined to intercede for their health or for their jobs. Worse, I am inclined to pray only for myself and my family! Grant me that eternal perspective that shows concern for their salvation, that shows concern for the spiritual blessings and values that can give meaning and purpose to life. Help me to be sensitive to the real needs of others, and make me aware of the heavenly blessings you want them to have; guide me by your indwelling Spirit to pray right for them and not just for myself. Amen.

O thou that hearest prayer, unto thee shall all flesh come.

Psalm 65:2

4
Intercession in the Plan of Redemption

God gave the world to man, made in His own image. He gave man the power to rule over it as a governor under Him. God planned that Adam should do nothing apart from Him, but everything with Him and through Him, that God himself would do all His work in the world through man. Adam was in very deed to be the owner, master, and ruler of the earth. When sin entered the world, Adam's power proved to be a terrible reality, for through him the earth, with the whole race of man, was brought under the curse of sin.

When God made the plan of redemption, His object was to restore man to the place from which he had fallen. God chose His servants of old so they could ask what they would and it should be given to them through the power of intercession for others. When Christ became a man, it was so He might intercede for man, as a man, both on earth and in heaven. Before Jesus left the world, He imparted this right of intercession to His disciples, so whatsoever they asked He would do for them (see John 15–17).

God's intense longing to bless seems in some sense to be graciously limited by His dependence on the intercession that rises from the earth. He seeks to rouse the spirit of intercession that He might be able to bestow His blessing on mankind. God regards intercession as the highest expression of His people's readiness to receive and to yield themselves wholly to the working of His almighty power.

Christians need to realize this as their true nobility and their only power with God: the right to claim and expect that God will hear prayer. It is only as God's children begin to see what intercession means with regard to God's kingdom that they will realize how solemn their responsibility is.

Each believer needs to see that God waits for him to take his part. He must feel in very truth that the highest, the most blessed, the mightiest of all human means for the fulfillment of the petition "as in heaven, so on earth" is the intercession that rises day and night, pleading with God for the power of heaven to be sent down into the hearts of men. Oh, that God might burn into our hearts this one thought: *Intercession in its omnipotent power is according to His will and is most certainly effectual!*

The Practice of Intercession

Permit me to remind you of the high example of your Master. Jesus Christ must be your pattern. Follow His leadership. Was there even one who interceded as He did? Remember His prayer in John 17: "Father, keep them, keep them from the evil!" Oh, what a prayer that was! He seems to have thought of all our needs, of all our weaknesses. In one long stream of intercession, He pours out His heart before His Father's throne. Oh, remember your Savior's example today. For there before the throne, with out-stretched hands, He prays. He prays not for himself, for He has attained His glory, but for us. He rests from His labors, for He has purchased us with His blood. For as many as are called by His grace, yes, and for those who shall believe on Him through our word:

> For all that come to God by Him,
> Salvation He demands;
> Points to the wounds upon His heart,
> And spreads His bleeding hands.

With such an example as this, we are very guilty if we forget to plead for others.

While we might continue to commend the duty of intercession by quoting numerous examples from the lives of eminent saints, it is enough for the true disciple of Christ to know that Christ in His holy Word made it our duty and privilege to intercede for others. When He taught us to pray, He said, "*Our* Father," and the expressions that follow are not in the singular but in the plural; for example, "Give *us* this day our daily bread."

If the Bible contained no command or example of intercessory prayer, the very spirit of Christianity would still constrain us to plead for others. Do you pray and, in the face and presence of God, think only of yourself? Surely if this is the case, the love of Christ is not in you, for the Spirit of Christ is not selfish. No one can live only for himself when once he has the love of Christ in him.

*D*ear Father in heaven, forgive me when I have prayed only selfishly, without any concern for others and the salvation of multitudes. Help me to realize clearly that my prayers do make a difference, that in some cases my prayers will be the deciding factor in your work being done in the way you would prefer. Thank you for trusting me with great power: work in me and through me in my prayers. Amen.

He saw that there was no man, and wondered that there was no intercessor.

Isaiah 59:16

5
God Seeks Intercessors

*F*rom days of old, God had intercessors among His people. He listened to their voices and gave deliverance. In Isaiah, we read of a time of trouble when God sought in vain for an intercessor. And He wondered! Think of what that means—the amazement of God that there should be no one who loved the people enough or who had sufficient faith in His power to deliver to intercede on their behalf. If there had been an intercessor, God could have given deliverance; without an intercessor His judgments came down (see Isa. 64:7; Ezek. 22:30, 31).

The place of the intercessor is infinitely important in the kingdom of God. Is it not indeed a matter of wonder that God should give people such power and yet so few know what it is to take hold of His strength and pray down His blessing on the world?

Let us try to realize the position. When God had in His Son wrought out the new creation and Christ had taken His place on the throne, the work of the extension of His kingdom was given into the hands of people. He ever lives to pray; prayer is the highest exercise of His royal prerogative as Priest-King upon the throne. All that Christ was to do in heaven was to be in fellowship with His people on earth. In His divine condescension, God has willed that the working of His Spirit shall follow the prayer of His people. He waits for their intercession, showing their preparation of heart—to what extent they are ready to yield to His Spirit.

God rules the world and His church through the prayers of His people. "That God should have made the extension of His kingdom to such a large extent dependent on the faithfulness of His people in prayer is a stupendous mystery and yet an absolute certainty." God calls for intercessors: in His grace He has made His work dependent on them; He waits for them.

The Practice of Intercession

It seems to me that when God gives any person much grace, it must be with the design that he may use it for the rest of the family. There is a heavenly patronage that you should use diligently. I pray you will use it on behalf of the poor, the sick, the afflicted, the tempted, the tried, the despondent, the despairing. When you have the King's ear, speak to Him on behalf of others.

When you are permitted to come very near to His throne, and He says to you, "Ask, and I will give you what you will"; when your faith is strong, your eye clear, your interest sure, and the love of God is sweetly shed abroad in your heart, then take the petitions of your poor brothers who stand outside at the gate and say, "My Lord, I have a poor brother, a poor child of yours, who has desired me to ask you a favor. Grant it to me. It shall be a favor to me. Grant it to him, for he is one of your own. Do it for Jesus' sake." You do not have a large measure of grace unless it prompts you to use your influence with God for others. If you have grace at all, and are not a mighty intercessor, then that grace must be but the size of a grain of mustard seed—a shriveled, ugly, puny thing.

You may have just enough grace to float your own soul clear of the quicksand, but no deep floods of grace, or you would carry in your joyous boat a rich cargo of the needs of others up to the throne of God. And you would bring back for others rich blessings that they could not have obtained except for you.

If you are like an angel, with your golden foot on the ladder that reaches to heaven; if you are ascending and descending, know that you will ascend with others' prayers and descend with others' blessings, for it is impossible for a full-grown saint to live or to pray for himself alone.

*D*ear Father, more often than I am aware my needs are being met through the prayers of others. I am thankful for this provision. Whenever I approach your throne of grace, I pray that your Holy Spirit will prompt me to pray for the needs of others. Remind me of any who have pressing needs, and encourage me with many answers to prayer. Amen.

He is able to save them to the uttermost that come unto God by him, seeing He ever liveth to make intercession for them.

(Hebrews 7:25).

6
Christ as Intercessor

When God had said in Isaiah that He wondered that there was no intercessor, there followed the words: "Therefore his arm brought salvation unto him. The Redeemer shall come to Zion" (Isa. 59:16, 20). God himself would provide the true intercessor, in Christ His Son, of whom it had already been said: "He bare the sin of many, and made intercession for the transgressors" (Isa. 53:12).

In His life on earth, Christ began His work as Intercessor. Think of the high priestly prayer on behalf of His disciples and all who should through them believe in His name. Think of His words to Peter, "I have prayed for thee, that thy faith fail not"—a proof of how intensely personal His intercession is. And on the cross He spoke as Intercessor: "Father, forgive them."

Now that He is seated at God's right hand, He continues, as our great High Priest, the work of intercession without ceasing. But with this difference: *He gives His people power to take part in His work of intercession.* Seven times in His farewell discourse, He repeated the assurance that what they asked He would do.

The power of heaven was to be at their disposal. The grace and power of God waited for man's bidding. Through the leading of the Holy Spirit, they would know what the will of God was. They would present their petition to the Father, and through His and their united intercession the Church would be clothed with the power of the Holy Spirit.

The Practice of Intercession

Remember that intercessory prayer is the sweetest prayer that God ever hears. Do not question it: the prayers of Christ are of this character. In all the incense that our Great High Priest now puts into the censor, there is not a single grain that is for himself. His work is done. His reward is obtained. Now, can you doubt that His prayers are the most acceptable of all supplications? The more your prayers are like Christ's, the more sweet they will be. While petitions for yourself will be accepted, your pleadings for others (having more in them of the fruits of the Spirit, more love, perhaps more faith, certainly more brotherly kindness) will be as the sweetest offerings you can give to God.

I can tell you that spiritually many have been given up for dead who were still within the reach of grace. There have been many who have been put into the spiritual burial shroud even by Christians, given up to damnation even by ministers, consigned to perdition even by their families. But into perdition they did not go because God found them and took them out of the horrible pit and out of the miry clay, and set their living feet upon the living rock.

Oh, give up on nobody! Pray still! Lay none out for spiritually dead until they are laid out naturally dead. But perhaps you say, "I cannot pray for others, for I am so weak and powerless." You will get strength, my brothers, by exertion. And besides, prevailing prayer does not depend solely upon the person who prays, but upon the power of the argument he uses. Now, if you sow seed you may be very feeble, but it is not your hand that puts the seed into the ground that produces the harvest: it is the vitality of the seed. And so in the prayer of faith. When you can plead a promise and drop that prayer into the ground with hope, your weakness shall not make it futile. Your prayer shall still prevail with God and bring down blessings from on high.

Job came from his dunghill to intercede for his friends. And so you may come from your couch of weakness. You may come from your poverty, your desertion, and intercede for others. Do not neglect intercessory prayer.

*D*ear Jesus, thank you for the encouragement to never give up on the eternal salvation of anyone. From my limited vision and finite perspective, I cannot see how you can reach into the hearts of some who have been so stubborn for so long, but I still pray that you might reach them with your grace before it is too late. Show me someone today who needs my prayers. For Jesus' sake. Amen.

I have set watchmen upon thy walls, O Jerusalem, they shall never hold their peace day nor night: ye that are Jehovah's remembrancers, take ye no rest and give him no rest.

Isaiah 62:6, 7 (A.S.V.)

7

The Intercessors God Seeks

Watchmen are ordinarily placed on the walls of a city to give notice to the rulers of coming danger. God appoints watchmen not only to warn people—often they will not hear—but also to summon Him to come to their aid whenever need or enemy may be threatening. The great mark of the intercessor is that he is not to hold his peace day or night, to take no rest, and to give God no rest, until the deliverance comes. In faith, he may count upon the assurance that God will answer his prayer.

Of intercessors our Lord Jesus said: "Shall not God avenge his own elect, who cry to him day and night?" From every land the voice is heard that the Christian Church, under the influence of the power of the world and the earthly-mindedness it brings, is losing its influence over its members. There is very little proof of God's presence in the conversion of sinners or the holiness of His people. With the great majority of Christians there is an utter neglect of Christ's call to take part in the extension of His kingdom. The power of the Holy Spirit is very little experienced.

Amid all the discussions as to what can be done to interest people, both young and old, in the study of God's Word, or to awaken love for the services of His house, one hears little of the indispensable necessity of the power of the Holy Spirit in the ministry and the membership of the Church. One sees very little sign of conviction and confession, and that is due to the lack of prayer. The workings of the Spirit are so feeble, and only by united fervent prayer can a change be brought about. If ever there was a time when God's elect should cry day and night to Him, it is now. Will you not, dear reader, offer yourself to God for this blessed work of intercession, and learn to count it the highest privilege of your life to be a channel through whose prayers God's blessing can be brought down to earth?

The Practice of Intercession

I commend the blessed privilege of intercession because of its sweet brotherly nature. You and I may be naturally hard and harsh and unlovely in spirit, but praying much for others will remind us we have, indeed, a relationship to the saints, that their interests are ours, that we are jointly concerned with them in the privilege of grace.

I do not know anything which, through the grace of God, may be a better means of uniting us the one to the other than constant prayer for each other. You cannot harbor animosity in your soul against your brother after you have learned to pray for him. If he has done you wrong, when you have taken that wrong to the mercy seat and prayed over it, you must forgive. Surely you could not be such a hypocrite as to invoke blessings on his head before God and then come forth to curse him in your own soul.

When there are complaints brought by brother against brother, it is generally the best to say, "Let us pray before we enter into this matter." Wherever there is a case to be decided by the pastor, he ought to say always to the brothers who contend, "Let us pray first." It will happen through prayer that the differences will soon be forgotten. They will become so slight, so trivial, that when the brothers rise from their knees they will say, "They are gone. We cannot contend now after having been one in heart before the throne of God."

If you will exercise yourselves much in supplication for your brothers, you will forgive their tempers, you will overlook their rashness, you will not think of their harsh words. But knowing that you also may be tempted and are of like passions with them, you will cover their faults and bear with their infirmities.

Dear Father, the Church is weak today because contention among members has replaced the unity of prayer and spirit. Help me to pray specifically today for those who are contentious. Keep me from unnecessary contention. Bring spiritual unity so our prayers can be heard. Amen.

Who in the days of his
flesh, when he had offered
up prayers and supplications
with strong crying and tears
. . . and was heard in that
he feared.

Hebrews 5:7

8
The School of Intercession

Christ, as Head, is Intercessor in heaven. We, as the members of His Body, are partakers with Him on earth. Let no one imagine that it cost Christ nothing to become an intercessor. He could not without a cost be our example. What do we read of Him? "When thou shalt make *his soul an offering for sin*, he shall see his seed. . . .I will divide him a portion with the great . . . because *he hath poured out his soul unto death*" (Isa. 53:10–12). Notice the thrice-repeated expression with regard to the pouring out of His soul.

The pouring out of His soul is the divine meaning of intercession. Nothing less than this was needed if His sacrifice and prayer were to have power with God His Father. This giving of himself over to live and die that He might save the perishing was a revelation of the spirit that has power to prevail with God.

If we as helpers and fellow laborers with the Lord Jesus are to share His power of intercession, there will need to be with us too the travail of soul that there was with Him, the giving up of our life and its pleasures for the one supreme work of interceding for our fellowmen. Intercession must not be a passing interest. It must become an ever-growing object of intense desire for which above everything we long and live. It is the life of consecration and self-sacrifice that will indeed give power for intercession (see Acts 15:26; 20:24; Phil. 2:17; Rev. 12:11).

The longer we study this blessed truth and think of what it means to exercise this power for the glory of God and the salvation of men, the deeper will become our conviction that it is worth giving up everything to take part with Christ in His work of intercession.

The Practice of Intercession

The salvation of sinners is a work in which everyone can aid. If I came to you and asked, "The Lord's cause requires money, what can you sacrifice for the Lord's work?" You might be compelled to answer, "The needs of my family do not permit me to do anything in that direction." But if I ask you to make the sacrifice of intercession neither you nor any Christian can say, "I cannot plead with God." If I were to press upon you at this moment the need of more public preaching, you might justly be excused, for some are slow of speech and have no gift for public speaking. But when it comes to interceding for saints and sinners, any Christian can fulfill the need. By praying, you can have a share in all the great works of the Church.

I have heard a holy woman say, "I cannot preach, but I can help my minister to preach by my prayers. Therefore, whenever I see him come into the pulpit, I will pray that

God will bless his words. So I have a share in what he does."

When you hear of a missionary working and making great sacrifices anywhere abroad, intercede for him and become a sacrificial co-worker. Beloved, some of you are often sickly in body, and during the weary night you get little sleep. Do you know why the Lord keeps you awake? So you can make the sacrifice of prayer. While others of us are sleeping, you are praying for us! God must have some to keep the night watches. He determines that a guard of prayer shall be set up around His Church all day and all night. You are the sentries of the night watches. Perhaps you cannot do anything else, but by praying you can obtain a share in the noblest works of the Church.

*D*ear Jesus, you sacrificed day and night for others. Teaching all day and praying all night, your crucifixion was the great culmination of your life of sacrifice. Forgive me when in my affluence I give money instead of prayers of intercession. Forgive me when in my poverty I sacrifice neither financially nor prayerfully. Rather than resenting their talents, help me to unite with those who have highly visible gifts, such as preaching and teaching, by praying for them and for their even greater success. Amen.

*H*itherto have ye asked nothing in my name. In that day ye shall ask in my name; ask, and ye shall receive, that your joy may be full.

John 16:24, 26

9

The Name of Jesus: The Power of Intercession

*D*uring Christ's life upon earth the disciples knew very little of the power of prayer in their own lives. In Gethsemane, Peter and the others utterly failed. They had no conception of what it was to ask in the name of Jesus and receive. The Lord promised them that in the future they would be able to pray with such a power in His name that they might ask what they would and it would be given to them.

"Hitherto . . . nothing." *"In that day* ye shall ask in my name . . . and shall receive." These two conditions are still found in the Church. With the great majority of Christians there is such a lack of knowledge of their oneness with Christ Jesus, and of the Holy Spirit as the Spirit of prayer, that they do not even attempt to claim the wonderful promises Christ gives here. But where God's children

know what it is to abide in Christ and to be in vital union with Him, and to yield to the Holy Spirit's teaching, they begin to learn that their intercession avails much and that God will give the power of His Spirit in answer to their prayer.

Faith in the power of Jesus' name and in our right to use it will give us the courage to follow on where God invites us to the holy office of intercessor. When our Lord Jesus, in His Farewell Discourse, gave His unlimited prayer promise, He sent the disciples out into the world with this consciousness: "He who sits upon the throne, and who lives in my heart, has promised that what I ask in His name I shall receive. *He will do it.*"

Oh, if Christians only knew what it is to yield themselves wholly and absolutely to Jesus Christ and His service, how their eyes would be opened to see that intense and unceasing prayerfulness is the essential mark of the healthy spiritual life; and that the power of all-prevailing intercession will indeed be the portion of those who live only in and for their Lord!

The Practice of Intercession

When he prayed, Moses employed the great name of God. How mightily did he argue with God on one occasion upon this ground! "What wilt thou do for thy great name? The Egyptians will say, Because the Lord could not bring them into the land, therefore he slew them in the wilderness." There are some occasions when the name of the Lord is very closely tied up with the history of His people. Sometimes in reliance upon a divine promise, a believer will be led to take a certain course of action.

Now, if the Lord should not be as good as His promise, not only is the believer deceived, but the wicked world looking on would say, "Aha! aha! Where is your God?" Take the case of our respected brother, Mr. Müller, of Bristol. These many years he has declared that God hears prayer, and firm in that conviction he has gone on to build house after house for the maintenance of orphans. Now, I can very well conceive that, if he were driven to a point of need for the maintenance of those thousand or two thousand children, he might very well use the plea, "What will you do for your great name?"

And you, in some severe trouble, when you have fairly received the promise, may say, "Lord, you have said, 'In six troubles I will be with thee, and in seven I will not forsake thee.' I have told my friends and neighbors that I put my trust in you, and if you do not deliver me now, where is thy name? Arise, O God, and do this thing, lest your honor be cast into the dust."

All the progress that is made by heretics and all the wrong things said by speculative atheists, and so on, should be used by Christians as an argument with God—why He should help the Gospel for His great name's sake.

Dear Jesus, for your name's sake bless missionaries, ministers, and churches around the world that are trying to be faithful to your Holy Word by their preaching, teaching, praying, and by being examples of your character. May they bear the fruits of the Holy Spirit, and may their work achieve visible success that you might be honored. Amen.

God hath sent forth the Spirit of his Son into your hearts, crying, Abba, Father.

Galatians 4:6

10
Prayer: The Work of the Spirit

We know what "Abba, Father" meant in the mouth of Jesus on Gethsemane. It meant the entire surrender of himself to death that the holy will of God's love in the redemption of sinners might be accomplished. In His prayer He was ready for any sacrifice, even to the yielding of His life. In that prayer, we have revealed to us the heart of Him whose place is at the right hand of God. From there He exercises the wonderful power of intercession and the power to pour down the Holy Spirit.

It is to breathe the very spirit of His Son into our hearts that the Holy Spirit has been bestowed by the Father. Our Lord would have us yield ourselves as wholly to God as He did; to pray like Him, that God's will of love should be done on earth at any cost. As God's love is revealed in His desire for the salvation of souls, so also the desire of Jesus was made plain when He gave himself for them. Now He asks for that same love to fill His people so they might give themselves wholly to the work of intercession and at any cost pray down God's love upon the perishing.

Lest anyone should think that this is too high and beyond our reach, the Holy Spirit is actually given into our hearts that we might pray as Jesus did, in His power, and in His name. The person who yields himself wholly to the leading of the Holy Spirit will feel urged by the compulsion of a divine love to an undivided surrender, to a life of continual intercession, because he knows that it is God who is working in him.

Now we can understand how Christ could give such unlimited promises to answer the prayers of His disciples. They were first going to be filled with the Holy Spirit. Now we understand how God can give such a high place to intercession in the fulfillment of His purpose of redemption. It is the Holy Spirit who breathes God's own desire into us and enables us to intercede for souls.

The Practice of Intercession

Faith is the first grace, the root of piety, the foundation of holiness, the dawn of godliness; to this faith must the first care be given. But we must not tarry at the first principles. Onward is our course. What then follows on the heels of faith? What is faith's firstborn child? When the vine of faith becomes vigorous and produces fruit unto holiness, what is the first ripe cluster? It is prayer—"praying in the Holy Spirit."

That man who has no faith has no prayer, and the man who abounds in faith will soon abound in intercession. All acceptable prayer must be in the Holy Spirit. Prayer that is not in the Holy Spirit is in the flesh. That which is born of the flesh is flesh, and we are told that they which are in the flesh cannot please God. The seed of acceptable devotion must come from heaven's storehouse. Only the prayer that comes from God can go to God. The dove will bear a letter only to the home from which it came. So, prayer will go back to heaven if it came down from heaven. We must shoot the Lord's arrows back to Him. That desire which He writes upon our hearts will move His heart and bring down a blessing, but the desires of the flesh have no power with Him.

I beseech you to examine yourself with rigorous care. Use the verse, "praying in the Holy Spirit," as a refining pot, a furnace, a touchstone, or a crucible by which to discern whether your prayers have been true or not. For this is the test: Has your praying in very deed been "praying in the Holy Spirit"?

*D*ear Heavenly Father, thank you for providing everything I need to offer acceptable prayer to you. Thank you for your Word with its sure guide to your promises, and thank you for your indwelling Holy Spirit, who will place your desires into my heart and empower me to offer prevailing prayer for your will to be done. Make me aware of any praying that I might do in the flesh, and remind me to pray in faith through the Holy Spirit. Touch my heart today. Draw me close to you. For Jesus' sake. Amen.

He shall divide the spoil with the strong, because . . . he bare the sin of many, and made intercession for the transgressors.

Isaiah 53:12

11
Christ: Our Example in Intercession

*H*e made intercession for the transgressors." What did that mean to Him? Think of what it cost Him to pray that prayer effectually. He had to pour out His soul as an offering for sin, and to cry in Gethsemane: "Father, Thy holy will of love be done."

Think what moved Him to sacrifice himself to the very uttermost! He loved His Father and wanted His holiness to be manifest. He loved souls and wanted them to be partakers of His holiness.

Think of the reward He won! As conqueror of every enemy, He is seated at the right hand of God with the power of unlimited and assured intercession. Now He sees His seed, a generation of those with the same mind as His, whom He trains to share in His great work of intercession.

What does this mean for us, when we indeed seek to pray for the transgressors? It means that we, too, must yield ourselves wholly to the glory of the holiness and the love of the Father. We, too, must pray: "Thy will be done, cost what it may. We, too, will sacrifice ourselves, even to pouring out our souls unto death."

The Lord Jesus has in very deed taken us up into partnership with himself in carrying out the great work of intercession. He in heaven and we on earth must have one mind, one aim in life: we should from love to the Father and to the lost consecrate our lives to intercession for God's blessing. The burning desire of Father and Son for the salvation of souls must be the burning desire of our heart too.

What an honor! What a blessedness! What a power for us to do the work! Because He lives, His Spirit pours forth His love into our hearts!

The Practice of Intercession

The prophet Jeremiah prayed with an amazing holy boldness after God had explicitly commanded, "Pray not for this people for their good." After praying with God, his heart grew so warm with sacred fervor and his spirit became so fired with passionate zeal that he could not help pleading for the sinful nation. He poured out his soul in passionate prayer to the Lord: "We will wait upon thee" (Jer. 14).

Perhaps this was disobedience in the outward form. But it was not disobedience in the inner spirit of the prophet. For the Lord does not count as disobedience the earnest pleadings and yearnings of the heart of His people. Jeremiah records a marvelous instance where under the most discouraging circumstances, when there appears no prospect whatever of success, people are moved by God to pray for their fellows and still intercede on behalf of those who are altogether unworthy of their supplications.

Do you see the beauty of the true intercessor? Endeavor by the power of God's Spirit to imitate the intercessor. Jeremiah interceded for the people. In infinite mercy, God gave the weeping prophet to His sinful people in order that they might not be left as sheep without a shepherd and be given over to destruction.

Whenever you meet a person who intercedes with God for his fellowmen, and makes this the main business of his life, you see in him one of the most precious gifts of God's grace to the age in which he lives. *God writes intercession upon our hearts.* All true prayer comes from God, but especially that least selfish and most Christlike form of prayer called intercession: when the petitioner forgets all about himself and his own needs, and all his pleadings, tears, and arguments are on behalf of others.

*D*ear Father, as I read these meditations on intercessory prayer, it is so easy for me to begin thinking more about myself and how I measure up to these thoughts rather than actually asking for the gift of intercession for the benefit of others. I live in a needy world, see a needy Church, and know many needy people. Fill me with the spirit of intercession for their behalf, and help me to focus my prayer efforts toward others and not just myself. Amen.

*T*hy will be done.

Matthew 26:42

12
God's Will and Ours

*T*he high prerogative of God is that everything in heaven and earth is to be done according to His will and as the fulfillment of His desires. When He made us in His image it was, above all, that our desires were to be in perfect accord with His desires. The high honor of being in the likeness of God is that we are to feel and wish just as God. In human flesh we are to be the embodiment and fulfillment of God's desires.

When God created man with the power of willing and choosing what he should be, He chose to limit himself in the exercise of His own will. When man fell and yielded himself to the will of God's enemy, God in His infinite love set about the great work of winning mankind back, to making the desires of God man's own desires. As in God, so in man, desire is the great moving power. Since man had yielded himself to a life of desire after the things of the earth and the flesh, God had to redeem him and to educate him into a life of harmony with himself. His one aim was that our desire should be in perfect accord with His own desire.

The great step in this direction was made when the Son of God came into this world to reproduce the divine desires in His human nature. He prayed and yielded himself up to the perfect fulfillment of all that God wished and willed. The Son of God, as man, said in agony and blood, "Thy will be done." He made the surrender even to the point of being forsaken by God that the power which had deceived man might be conquered and deliverance procured. The wonderful and complete harmony between the Father and the Son was manifested when the Son said, "Thy will of love be done," so the great redemption could be accomplished.

Now the great work of appropriating that redemption is this: Believers must say, first of all for themselves and then in lives devoted to intercession for others, "Thy will be done on earth as it is in heaven." As we plead for the Church, its ministers and its missionaries, its strong Christians and its new converts, for the unsaved (whether nominally Christian or heathen), we have the privilege of knowing that we are *pleading for what God wills*, and that through our prayers His will is to be done on earth as it is in heaven.

The Practice of Intercession

We do not always know what to pray for, and if we were to refrain from prayer for a few minutes until we did know, it would be a good and wise rule. The habit into which we have fallen in extemporaneous praying, of always praying immediately after we are asked without a moment's pause in which to think of what we are going to ask, is very harmful to the spirit of prayer.

I like to take a few minutes to consider what I am going to ask of God. Otherwise it is like seeking an interview with one of the officers of the state to ask for some-thing that has just occurred to you. Surely common sense would say, "Wait awhile until you have your case mapped out in your own mind, and then when you clearly know yourself what it is that you want, you will be able to ask for what you need."

Should we not wait upon God in prayer, asking Him to reveal to us what those matters are concerning which we should plead with Him? Beware of hit-and-miss pray-ers. Never make haphazard work of intercession. Come to the throne of grace intelligently, understanding what it is that you require.

We feel secure when the Holy Spirit guides our minds. But many spiritual people consciously feel themselves boxed in regarding certain matters, and are free to pray in only one direction. Let them obey the Holy Spirit and pray as He directs, for He knows what our petitions should be. Pray for what the Holy Spirit moves you to pray, and be very sensitive to His influence.

Come Holy Spirit, I wait upon you now, I ask you to quiet my mind, to reveal to me the will of God and who and what things I am to pray for now. I will not rush away but will pray for whatever you desire in Jesus' name. Amen.

I have set watchmen upon thy walls, O Jerusalem; they shall never hold their peace day nor night: ye that are Jehovah's remembrancers, take ye no rest and give him no rest.

Isaiah 62:6, 7 (A.S.V.)

13

The Blessedness of a
Life of Intercession

What an unspeakable grace to be allowed to deal with God in intercession for the supply of the needs of others!

What a blessing, in close union with Christ, to take part in His great work as Intercessor, and to mingle my prayers with His! What an honor to have power with God in heaven over souls, and to obtain for them what they do not know or think!

What a privilege as a steward of the grace of God to bring to Him the state of the Church or of individual lives, of the ministers of the Word or of His messengers away in heathendom, and plead on their behalf till He entrusts me with the answer!

What blessedness, in union with other Christians, to strive together in prayer until the victory is gained over difficulties here on earth or over the powers of darkness in high places!

It is indeed worth living: to know that God will use

me as an intercessor to receive and dispense here on earth His heavenly blessing, and above all the power of His Holy Spirit.

The very life of heaven, the life of the Lord Jesus himself, in His self-denying love, can take possession of me and urge me to yield myself wholly to bear the burden of souls before Him and to plead that they may live.

For too long we have thought of prayer simply as a means for supplying our needs in life and service. May God help us see what a place intercession takes in His divine counsel and in His work for the kingdom. May our hearts feel that there is no honor or blessedness on earth equal to the unspeakable privilege of waiting upon God and bringing down from heaven and opening the way on earth for the blessings He delights to give!

The Practice of Intercession

I like the metaphor of the man who said that he wished his own mind to be as a cork upon the water, conscious of every motion of the Holy Spirit. It is well to be so sensitive to the Spirit of God that His faintest breath would cause a ripple upon the sea of our souls and make us move as the Spirit wills. We have reached a high state of sanctification when God the Spirit and our own inward spirit are in perfect accord. May we be led into that unspeakably blessed state!

If we think only of what *we* want and *we* wish for, and then ask for it selfishly, we do not pray rightly. To pray rightly, we must consent to the mind of the Spirit and speak as He moves us to speak. We shall surely be enriched with good things when we wait for Him to give us the very matter of our petitions. "Lord, teach us to pray. Put the thoughts into our minds, the desires into our hearts, and the very words into our mouths, if it be your will, so that all through our praying we will be praying in the Spirit and not in the flesh."

The main part of praying in the Spirit must not lie merely in the Spirit's power, or in the Spirit's teaching us what to pray for, but in the Spirit's assisting us *in the manner* of prayer. There are many obnoxious ways of praying to God. There is only one *manner* of praying that God accepts. You know what it is: the one who comes to God must remember that He is "a Spirit, and they that worship him must worship him in spirit and in truth, for the Father seeketh such to worship him." The very first essential of prayer is to pray *in truth*. We do not pray in truth unless the Spirit of God leads our minds into the sincerity and reality of devotion. To pray in truth is to mean what we say, for the heart to agonize with God and heave with strong desires. Only a spiritual man moved by the Holy Spirit will find this manner of prayer.

*D*ear Father, what a blessed experience it is to pray in union with you and your Son through the presence of your Holy Spirit in my mind and heart. What a joy it is to intercede with others for others according to your will. Grant us more precious time together in prayer. Amen.

These all continued with one accord in prayer and supplication.

Acts 1:14

14
The Place of Prayer

*T*he last words Christ spoke before He left the world give us the four great notes of His church: "Wait for the promise of the Father. . . . Ye shall receive power after that the Holy Spirit is come upon you. . . . Ye shall be witnesses unto me. . . . Both in Jerusalem and unto the uttermost part of the earth."

United and unceasing prayer, the power of the Holy Spirit, living witnesses to the living Christ, from Jerusalem to the uttermost part of the earth—such are the marks of the true Gospel, of the true ministry, of the true Church of the New Testament.

A church of united and unceasing prayerfulness, a ministry filled with the Holy Spirit, with members living witnesses to a living Christ, with a message to every creature on earth—such was the church that Christ founded, and such was the church that went out to conquer the world.

After Christ ascended to heaven, the disciples knew at once what their work was to be: *continuing with one accord in prayer and supplication.* They were bound together into one Body by the love and Spirit of Christ. This gave them their wonderful power with God and with people.

Their one duty was to wait in united and unceasing prayer for the power of the Holy Spirit, who would bring the enduement of power from on high for their witness to the ends of the earth. A praying church, a Spirit-filled church, a witnessing church, with all the world as its sphere and aim—such is the Church of Jesus Christ.

As long as the Church maintained this character it had power to conquer. But alas, as it came under the influence of the world, it lost much of its heavenly, supernatural beauty and strength! How unfaithful in prayer, how feeble the workings of the Spirit, how formal its witness to Christ, and how unfaithful to its worldwide mission!

The Practice of Intercession

The first meeting for prayer that we find after our Lord's ascension to heaven is the one mentioned at the beginning of this chapter. From that meeting, we learn that united prayer is the comfort of a disconsolate church. Can you judge the sorrow that filled the hearts of the disciples when their Lord was gone? They were an army without a leader, a flock without a shepherd, a family without a head. Exposed to innumerable trials, the strong wall of His presence was now withdrawn. In the deep desolation of their spirits, they resorted to united prayer. They were like a flock of sheep that will huddle together in a storm.

These first disciples felt that nothing made them so happy, nothing so gave them boldness, nothing so strengthened them to bear their daily difficulties as drawing near to God in common intercession.

Let every church learn the value of its prayer meetings in its dark hour. When the pastor has died, and it is difficult to find a successor; when there are divisions in the church; when poverty comes; when there is spiritual famine; when the Holy Spirit seems to have withdrawn himself—there is only one remedy for these and a thousand evils: a united prayer: "Let *us* pray."

The churches that are slowly dwindling might soon restore their numbers if they knew how to pray. Though they are dispirited now, defeat would soon become success, their spirits would be revived by drawing near to God. And if you are afflicted or troubled, you shall find that after going to the house of God for prayer, your own private place of prayer will particularly comfort you again. Come and unite with the saints of God in prayer, and you will see the footsteps of the Shepherd in the flock, and soon you shall see the Shepherd himself. United prayer will encourage discouraged people.

*D*ear Father, make me more sensitive to your Spirit, more aware of the desires of your Spirit within me. Give me power in prayer and power with people as I seek to proclaim and do only your will always. Teach me whom to pray for as I seek to lead others to saving faith in Jesus Christ. Amen.

I bow my knees unto the
Father, that he would grant
you to be strengthened with
might by his
Spirit.

Ephesians 3:14, 16

15

Paul as an Intercessor

We think of Paul as the great missionary, the great preacher, the great writer, the great apostle "in labors more abundant." We do not think sufficiently of him as the intercessor, who sought and obtained the power that rested upon all his other activities and brought down the blessing that rested upon the churches he served.

We see from our text what he wrote to the Ephesians. Think of what he said to the Thessalonians: "Night and day *praying exceedingly*, that we might perfect that which is lacking in your faith, to the end he may establish your hearts unblamable in holiness" (1 Thess. 3:10, 13). To the Romans he wrote: "Without ceasing I make mention of you always *in my prayers*" (Rom. 1:9). To the Philippians he declared: "Always *in every prayer* of mine for you all, making request with joy" (Phil. 1:4). And to the Colossians he said: "We do not cease *to pray* for you. I would that ye knew what great conflict I have for you" (Col. 1:9; 2:1).

Day and night he cried to God in his intercession for them, that the light and the power of the Holy Spirit might be in them. As earnestly as he believed in the power of his intercession for them, so also he believed in the blessing that their prayers would bring upon him. "I beseech you, that ye strive together with me in your prayers to God for me" (Rom. 15:30). "God will yet deliver us, ye also helping together by prayer for us" (2 Cor. 1:10, 11). "Praying also for me, that I may open my mouth boldly" (Eph. 6:18, 19; Col. 4:3; 2 Thess. 3:1). "This shall turn to my salvation through your prayer" (Phil. 1:19).

The whole relationship between pastor and people depends on their united continual prayerfulness. Their whole relationship to each other is heavenly, spiritual and divine, and can be maintained only by unceasing prayer. When ministers and people become aware that the power and blessing of the Holy Spirit is waiting for their united and unceasing prayer, then the Church will begin to know something of what apostolic Christianity is.

The Practice of Intercession

Every child of God must pray for the rest of the Christian family. The new nature created within us by the Holy Spirit teaches us this. Didn't you find that as soon as you possessed divine life, you began without any exhortation to pray for others? Your very first believing cries began with "*Our* Father which art in heaven," and so included others besides you.

Among the earliest prayers a renewed heart will offer will be a prayer for the person through whose agency he was brought to Jesus. No new convert forgets to pray for the minister or the layman who was the instrument of his conversion.

A newly delivered person will also plead for others who are still in the deplorable condition from which grace has enabled him to escape. "You have brought my soul out

of prison, Lord, set my fellow captives free. In your lov-
ingkindness enable others to taste the sweetness of salvation through you." And Christian people, who have at any
time conversed with the convert, who have ministered to
his comfort or instruction, will be sure to obtain a share
in his prayers; for a renewed heart is a tenderly grateful
heart. A person is not truly born from above unless he feels
thankfulness for his earnest Christian friends below.

Set a bird free from a cage, and it will sing you its
thanks as it speeds forth into the air. Even thus, if you are
enabled to open the prison doors of bondaged individuals,
they will repay your loving efforts with prayer.

Dear Jesus, thank you for raising up Christian
friends and ministers to pray for me that I might be saved.
Today, I want to remember many whom I know by name,
and intercede with thanksgiving in their behalf. I also thank
you for those unknown to me, who have supported me
through their prayers, and I ask you to bless them for your
sake. Amen.

The harvest truly is plenteous, but the laborers are few; pray ye therefore the Lord of the harvest, that he will send forth laborers into his harvest.

Matthew 9:37, 38

16

Intercession for Laborers

*T*he disciples understood very little of what these words meant. Christ gave them as a seed-thought to be lodged in their hearts for later use. At Pentecost, as they saw how many of the new converts were ready in the power of the Spirit to testify of Christ, they must have felt how the ten days of continuous united prayer had brought this blessing too, as the fruit of the Spirit's power—laborers in the harvest.

Christ meant to teach us that however large the field may be, and however few the laborers, prayer is the best, the sure, the only means for supplying the need.

What we need to understand is that it is not only in time of need that the prayer must be sent up, but that the whole work is to be carried on in the spirit of prayer, so that the prayer for laborers shall be in perfect harmony with the whole of our life and effort.

In the China Inland Mission, when the number of missionaries had gone up to 200 at a conference held in China, they felt so deeply the need of more laborers for districts quite unprovided for that, after much prayer, they felt at liberty to ask God to give them within a year 100 additional laborers and 10,000 pounds to meet the expenses. They agreed to continue in prayer day by day throughout the year. At the end of the time, the 100 suitable men and women had been found and 11,000 pounds had been given.

To meet the need of the world, its open fields and its waiting souls, the churches all complain of the lack of laborers and of funds to support them. Does not Christ's voice call us to the united and unceasing prayer of the first disciples? God is faithful, by the power of His Spirit, to supply every need. Let the Church take the posture of united prayer and supplication. God hears prayer.

The Practice of Intercession

What an honor for us, who so lately were beggars for ourselves at mercy's door, to receive so much of the royal favor that we may venture to speak a word in the King's ear for others. Sovereign mercy allowed us to say, "Have mercy upon me!" Now we can come to the Lord and pray, "I would like to speak a word with you for a brother of mine. I would venture to ask bounties from your hands, my Father, for a sister who needs compassion." See how eminently you are promoted: you are ordained to the high office of "the King's remembrancers," to ask Him about the good things of His covenant. You are appointed a royal distributor of alms for the King of kings. He sets before you His open treasury, and bids you to ask what you will.

Oh, priceless grace! If you, O believer, know how to ask by faith, you may hand out to your brothers and sisters wealth more precious than the gold of King Solomon. Intercession is the key of the ivory palaces, wherein are contained the boundless treasures of God. In intercession, saints of God reach a place where angels cannot stand. The angels rejoice over repentant sinners, but we do not read of their being admitted as intercessors for the saints. Yet we, as imperfect as we are, have this favor. We are permitted to open our mouths before the Lord for the sick and the tried, for the troubled and the downcast, with the assurance that whatsoever we ask in prayer believing, we shall receive. In this, great honor has been placed upon you.

If I pray for the brethren, I remember that Christ stands before the throne of glory. Is it not a delightful thing to be partakers with the Son of God in the ministry of intercession? In this service, He has made us priests unto our God. Beloved, if you would be conformed in service to the Lord Jesus, be much in intercession for the saints.

*D*ear Heavenly Father, I come before you today and ask that you release from your great storehouse of treasures many gifts for your struggling ministers, missionaries, and saints around the world. Grant them all their spiritual and material needs as your faithful servants. Amen.

Y e shall be gathered one by one, O ye children of Israel.

Isaiah 27:12

17
Intercession for Individual Souls

*I*n our body every member has its appointed place. It is also true in society and in the Church. The work must always aim at the welfare and the highest perfection of the whole through the cooperation of every individual member.

In the Church the thought is found too often that the salvation of people is the work of the minister; whereas, he generally deals only with the crowd, but seldom reaches the individual. This is the cause of a twofold evil. The individual believer does not understand that it is necessary for him to testify to those around him—for the nourishment and the strengthening of his own spiritual life and for the ingathering of souls. Unconverted people suffer unspeakable loss because Christ is not personally brought to them by each believer they meet. The thought of intercession for those around us is all too seldom found. Restoration of its right place in the Christian life—how much that would mean to the Church and its missions!

Oh, when will Christians learn the great truth that "what God in heaven desires to do *needs prayer on earth as its indispensable condition*"? As we realize this we shall see that intercession is the chief element in the conversion of souls. All our efforts are vain without the power of the Holy Spirit given in answer to prayer. When ministers and their people unite in a covenant of prayer and testimony, the Church will flourish and every believer will understand the part he has to take.

And what can we do to stir up the spirit of intercession? First, let every Christian, as he begins to get an insight into the need and the power of intercession, make a beginning in the exercise of it on behalf of single individuals. Pray for your children, for your relatives and friends, for all with whom God brings you into contact. If you feel that you have not the power to intercede, let the discovery humble you and drive you to the mercy seat in prayer. *God wants every redeemed child of His to intercede for the perishing.* It is the vital breath of the normal Christian life—the proof that a person is truly born from above.

Then pray intensely and persistently that God may give the power of His Holy Spirit to you and His children around you that the power of intercession may have the place God will honor.

The Practice of Intercession

Pledge yourself to be more persistent in prayer for sinners all around you. Like Abraham, a great city is before you; plead for it. Like Moses, you dwell among a sinful people; stand in the gap for them. I charge you by your allegiance to God, if indeed you are not a liar in your profession that He is your Lord, to pray persistently for the ungodly, every individual sinner you know, that they might be brought to Jesus.

Plead with God, He loves your prayers. Your intercessory prayers are like the sweet incense upon the golden altar. Plead with Him, and you shall live to see a reward for your pleadings in the conversion of the sons of men.

Make your children the special objects of your afternoon's cries. Implore the Lord to save your husband or your wife, your father or your mother, and your nearest neighbor. Implore a blessing upon each person who attends your church, and especially upon those who are unregenerate. Pray for those on the street where you live, for those in the district where you live, and ask for a gracious visitation from the Lord.

I saw four men converted to the Lord, but their wives were not. These four men met together for united prayer in behalf of their wives, and their four spouses were brought to the Lord. Anything is possible for those who believe. May God help you to believe and intercede!

*D*ear Father, increase my belief in prayer. Place one special person on my heart today, a person you want to save. Hear my daily persistent prayers for that person, and save them that we might see your glory, in Jesus' name. Amen.

And for me . . . praying also for us. . . . Finally, brethren, pray for us.

Ephesians 6:19; Colossians 4:3; 2 Thessalonians 3:1

18

Intercession for Ministers

*T*hese expressions of Paul suggest what the strength of his conviction must have been: Christians have power with God, and their prayers would indeed bring new strength to him in his work. He had such a sense of the actual unity of the Body of Christ, of the interdependence of each member, on the life that flowed through the whole Body, that he sought to rouse Christians, both for their own sakes and for his sake, and for the sake of the Kingdom of God, with his call: "Continue in prayer, and watch in the same with thanksgiving, withal praying also for us."

The Church depends upon the ministry to an extent we very little realize. The place of the minister is so high, as the steward of the mysteries of God, as the ambassador for God to beseech people in Christ's name to be reconciled to Him, that unfaithfulness or inefficiency must bring a terrible blight on the Church he serves. If Paul, after having preached for twenty years in the power of God, still needed the prayers of the Church, how much more does the ministry in our day need them?

The minister needs the prayers of his people. He has a right to them. He is in truth dependent upon them. *It is his task to train Christians for their work of intercession on behalf of the Church and the world.* He must begin by training them to pray for him. He may have to begin still further back and learn to pray more for himself and for them. Let all intercessors who are seeking to enter more deeply into their blessed work give a larger place to the ministry, whether of their own church or of other churches.

Let them plead with God for individual people and for special circles. Let them continue in prayer and watch therein that ministers may be men of power, men of prayer, and full of the Holy Spirit. Oh, brothers and sisters in Christ, pray . . . pray for the ministry!

The Practice of Intercession

Paul tells us to learn more about those who labor among us and are over us in the Lord. I wish all church members did know more of their pastor's struggles, sorrows, and joys that they might have more sympathy with him. The more you know and sympathize, the better your prayers will be.

Earnest intercession will be sure to bring love with it. I do not believe you can hate a person for whom you habitually pray. If you dislike any brother in Christ, pray for him doubly—not only for his sake, but also for yours, that you may be cured of prejudice and saved from all unkind feeling.

Remember the old story of the person who waited for his pastor after service to tell him that he could not enjoy his preaching. The minister wisely replied, "My dear brother, before we talk the matter over, let us pray together." After they both had prayed, the complainer found he had nothing to say, except to confess that he himself had been very negligent in prayer for his pastor, and laid that as the cause for his not benefiting from the pastor's sermons.

I ascribe the lack of brotherly love to the decline of intercessory prayer. Pray for one another earnestly, habitually, fervently, and you will knit your hearts together in love as the heart of one person.

When you pray for one another, not only will your sympathy and love grow, but you will have kinder judgments concerning one another. We always judge leniently those for whom we pray. If a talebearer and gossip represents my brother in a very black light, my love makes me feel sure he is mistaken. Did I pray for him this morning. Then how can I hear him condemned? If I am compelled to believe that he is guilty, I am very sorry; but I will not be angry with him, I will pray for the Lord to forgive and restore him to righteousness and favor.

Dear Father, create in me a clean heart, put a right spirit within me, and help me love every person as you love. Help me to see others as you see them, and help me pray for all people as you would have me pray. Join my heart in love with all those who are committed to your cause. Amen.

With all prayer and supplication praying at all seasons in the Spirit, and watching thereunto in all perseverance and supplication for all the saints.

Ephesians 6:18

19
Prayer for All Saints

Notice how Paul repeats words in the intensity of his desire to reach the hearts of his readers. "With *all* prayer and supplication praying at *all* seasons, watching thereunto in *all* perseverance and *all* supplication." He says, "All prayer . . . all seasons . . . all perseverance . . . all supplication." The words claim thought if they are to meet with the needed response.

Paul felt so deeply the unity of the Body of Christ, and was so sure that the unity could be realized only in the exercise of love and prayer, that he pleaded with the believers at Ephesus unceasingly and fervently to pray for all saints, not only in their immediate circle, but for all in the Church of Christ of whom they might hear. "Unity is strength." As we exercise this power of intercession with all perseverance, we shall be delivered from self with all its feeble prayers, and lifted up to that enlargement of heart in which the love of Christ can flow freely and fully through us.

Often the great lack in true believers is that in prayer they are occupied with themselves and with what God must do for them. Let us realize that we have here a call to every believer to give himself without ceasing to the exercise of love and prayer. It is as we forget ourselves, in the faith that God will take charge of us, and yield ourselves to the great and blessed work of calling down the blessing of God on our brethren, that the whole Church will be fitted to do its work in making Christ known to every creature. This alone is the healthy and the blessed life of a child of God who has yielded himself wholly to Christ Jesus.

Pray for God's children and the church around you. Pray for all the work in which they are engaged, or ought to be. Pray at all seasons in the Spirit for all God's saints. There is no blessedness greater than that of abiding communion with God. And there is no way that leads to the enjoyment of this more surely than the life of intercession for which these words of Paul appeal so pleadingly.

The Practice of Intercession

As intercessory prayer is an instinct of the heaven-born nature of the believer, so it is a law of the elect household of faith. Christians in their due order may be described as "praying always with all prayer and supplication in the Spirit, and watching thereunto with all perseverance and supplication for all saints." Every believer has a watchman's place appointed to him in the matter of prayer. He is bound not to be silent but to give the Lord no rest until He establishes and makes His people a praise upon the earth. Our prosperity is made to hinge upon intercessory prayer.

The new commandment the Lord has given us, in which He bids us to "love one another," necessitates our praying for each other. How can a person claim to love his brother if he never intercedes with God for him? Can I live continually with my fellow believers and see their sorrows and never cry to God in their behalf? Can I observe their poverty, their tribulation, their temptation, their heaviness of heart, and yet forget them in my supplications? Can I see their work of faith and labor of love, and never implore a blessing upon them? Can I wrap myself within myself, and be indifferent to the cares of those who are my brothers and sisters in Christ? Impossible! I must belong to some other family than that of God, for in the family of love, common sympathy leads to constant intercession.

God forbid that we should sin against the Lord by ceasing to pray for our brethren. Every bee in the hive of the Church should bring in its own share of this honey from the common store.

*D*ear Father, make me so sensitive to those around me that I begin to look deeply into the real cause of their troubles; not to condemn, but so as to pray more effectively for them and perhaps be the answer to my own prayers. Amen.

When they had fasted and prayed, and laid their hands on them, they sent them away.

Acts 13:3

20
Missionary Intercession

Someone has remarked that "the supreme question of foreign missions is how to multiply the number of Christians who will individually and collectively wield the force of intercession for the conversion and transformation of men. Every other consideration and plan is secondary to that of wielding the forces of prayer.

"We take for granted that those who love this work and bear it upon their hearts will follow the scriptural injunction to pray unceasingly for its triumph. Such intercessors will not only pray in the morning watch and the hours of stated devotion, but in all times and seasons will make intercession that refuses to let God go until He crowns His workers with victory."

Missions have their root in the love of Christ, a love that was proved on the cross and now lives in our hearts. As people are so earnest in seeking to carry out God's plans for the natural world, so God's children should be at least as wholehearted in seeking to bring Christ's love to all mankind. Intercession is the chief means appointed by God to bring the great redemption within the reach of all.

Pray for the missionaries that the Christ-life may be clear and strong, that they may be people of prayer and filled with love, in whom the power of the spiritual life is made manifest.

Pray for the native Christians that they may know the glory of the mystery among the heathen, Christ in them the hope of glory.

Pray for the baptism classes and all the pupils in schools that the teaching of God's Word may be in power. Pray especially for the national pastors and evangelists that the Holy Spirit may fill them to be witnesses for Christ among their fellow-countrymen.

Pray, above all, for the Church, that it may be lifted out of its indifference and that every believer may be brought to understand that the one object of his life is to help make Christ King on the earth.

The Practice of Intercession

I feel certain that before the Reformation, there must have been hundreds of godly men and women who were day and night interceding with the Lord and giving Him no rest until He answered their supplications. Luther and the rest of the Reformers were sent by God in answer to the many prayers that history has never recorded, but which are written in the Lord's book of remembrance.

In more modern times, when Wesley and Whitefield stirred the smoldering embers of Christianity in England, it was because godly people, perhaps poor, obscure men and women in their cottages, reading the Scriptures, saw the sad state of irreligion and indifference into which the nation had fallen. They groaned and prayed and spread their case before God. I do not know how to estimate the worth of even one person who has power with God in prayer.

When John Knox pled for Scotland, it was the greatest event in Scottish history. All things are possible with a man who, like Elijah upon Carmel, casts himself down upon the earth, puts his face between his knees, and cries unto Him who hears prayer until the heavens that were like brass suddenly drop with plenteous showers of rain.

There is no power like that of intercession. The secret springs that move the puppets of earth—for kings and princes are often little more than that—are the prayers of God's believing people. Oh, if the Lord makes you an intercessor, even if you cannot speak with others for God, if you know how to speak with God for others, you occupy a position that is second to none. God help you fill it well!

*D*ear Lord Jesus, we will never know the full extent of our effectiveness in prayer until we look into your book of remembrance. Inspire us with your Holy Spirit to keep on praying, with groans that words cannot express, for missionaries around the world and for a genuine revival here in our own city and nation. Answer our prayers for your kingdom, even if it is one hundred years from now. Amen.

Continue in prayer, and watch in the same with thanksgiving, praying also for us.

Colossians 4:2, 3

21
The Grace of Intercession

*N*othing can bring us nearer to God and lead us deeper into His love than the work of intercession. Nothing can give us a higher experience of the likeness of God than the power of pouring out our hearts into the heart of God in prayer for people around us. Nothing can so closely link us to Jesus Christ, the great Intercessor, and give us the experience of His power and Spirit resting upon us, as the yielding of our lives to the work of bringing redemption into the hearts of our fellowmen. By intercession, we shall know more of the powerful working of the Holy Spirit, the prayer breathed by Him into our hearts, "Abba, Father," in all the fullness of meaning that it had for Christ in Gethsemane. Nothing can so help us prove the power and the faithfulness of God to His Word as reaching out in intercession to the multitudes, either in the Christian Church or in the darkness of heathenism. As we pour out our souls as a living sacrifice before God, with the one persistent plea that He shall in answer to our prayer open the windows of heaven and send down His abundant blessing, God will be glorified, our souls will reach their highest destiny, and God's kingdom will come.

Nothing will so help us understand and experience the living unity of the Body of Christ, and the irresistible power that it can exert, as the daily and continued fellowship with God's children in the persistent plea that God will arise and have mercy upon the Church and make her a light and a life to those who are sitting in darkness. Oh, my brother, how little we realize what we are losing in not living in fervent intercession! What may we not gain for ourselves and for the world if we allow the Holy Spirit, as a Spirit of grace and of supplication, to master our whole being!

In heaven Christ lives to pray. His whole conversation with His Father is prayer—an asking and receiving of the fullness of the Holy Spirit for His people. God delights in nothing so much as in prayer. Shall we not learn to believe that the highest blessings of heaven will be unfolded to us as we pray more?

The Practice of Intercession

Instead of saying to us, "If you cannot pray, you shall not have; if you have not grace enough to ask rightly, I will shut the gates of mercy against you," Jesus has devised a means by which He can bring the lame and the banished into His presence. He teaches the ignorant how to pray. He strengthens the weak with His own strength. Here He does wonders in the condescending assistance of God himself.

The Holy Spirit, the third person of the Trinity, helps our infirmities, making intercession for us with groanings that cannot be uttered. The mark of God's wonderful condescension is that He not only answers our prayers when they are made, but He makes our prayers for us. That God the King should say to us, "Bring your case before me, and I will grant your desire," is kindness. But for Him to also say, "I will be your secretary. I will write out your petition for you. I will put it into proper words and use fitting phrases so that your petition will be framed acceptably"; this is goodness stretched to the limit. The Holy Spirit does precisely this for us poor, ignorant, wavering, weak sons of men.

I understand the expression "praying in the Holy Spirit" to mean that the Holy Spirit is actually willing to help me pray, that He will tell me how to pray, and that when I get to a point where I am at a loss and cannot express my desires, He will appear in my extremity and make intercession for me with groanings that cannot be uttered.

God himself the Holy Spirit condescends to assist you in prayer. Perhaps if you cannot put two words together in common speech to men; yet, He will help you speak to God in prayer.

*D*ear Holy Spirit of God, there are many people and things I want to pray for, but I do not know how to pray for these effectively. I am at a loss for the keys to success. Please pray in and through me, and give me words from the heart that will bring victory for Jesus' sake. Amen.

There is one body, and one Spirit.

Ephesians 4:4

22
United Intercession

Our own bodies teach us how essential for their health and strength it is for every member to take its full share in seeking the welfare of the whole. Likewise, how true of the Body of Christ! There are, alas, too many who look upon salvation only in connection with their own happiness. There are those, again, who know that they live not unto themselves, and truly seek in prayer and work to bring others to share in their happiness. But some do not yet understand that in addition to their personal circle or church, they have a calling to enlarge their hearts to take the whole Body of Christ Jesus into their love and their intercession.

The Spirit and love of Christ will enable us to do this. Only when intercession *for the whole Church, by the whole Church* ascends to God's throne will the Spirit of unity and power have its full sway. The desire that has been awakened for closer union between the different branches of the Christian Church is cause for thanksgiving. And yet, the difficulties are so great and, in the case of different nationalities of the world so apparently insuperable, that the thought of a united Church on earth appears beyond reach.

Let us bless God that there is a unity in Christ Jesus deeper and stronger than any visible manifestation could make it. There is a way in which even now amid all diversity of administrations, the unity can be practically exemplified and utilized as the means of an unthought-of accession of divine strength and blessing in the work of the kingdom. *The cultivation and increase of the Spirit and the exercise of intercession will bring true unity.* As believers are taught the meaning of their calling as a royal priesthood, they are led to see that God is not confined in His love or promises to their limited spheres of labor but invites them to enlarge their hearts, and like Christ—we may say like Paul, too—to pray for all who believe or can yet be brought to believe that this earth and the Church of Christ in it will by intercession be bound to the throne of heaven as it has never been yet.

Let Christians and ministers of the Gospel agree and bind themselves together for this worldwide intercession. It will strengthen the confidence that prayer will be heard, and that their prayers, too, will become indispensable for the coming of the kingdom.

The Practice of Intercession

We recognize a vital union among believers, a oneness of a very intimate type. We are not merely brethren, but we are "members of the same body." Christ is the head of His mystical body the Church, and we are members of His body.

Just as in the human body, each limb, organ, vein, nerve, is needful to the whole; so in the Church, each believer is necessary to the rest. We may not be able to show what particular mischief would be done to the arm by an injury to the knee. Yet, rest assured, there would be sympathetic suffering. No single cell within the whole body can be out of order without in some degree affecting all the rest.

God made us dependent upon one another far more than we imagine. In the Church, each person contributes to the health or to the disease of the whole body, and he cannot avoid doing so. When a believer grows in grace, he is enriched, and the whole Christian community increases by the spiritual wealth he gains. On the other hand, when a person declines in divine things, and so becomes spiritually poor and feeble, he is injured and in a measure the Church is impoverished, weakened, and injured. Since this is the case, let us discharge abundantly the duties that we owe to the Body; and in the delightful exercise of intercession, let us abound more and more.

A prayerless church member is a hindrance. He is like a rotting bone or a decayed tooth, and will become a sorrow and danger to the Body of Christ.

*F*ather, help me to appreciate the importance of my prayers for the Church, and never let me be the reason for the presence of any disease in your Body. Amen.

*P*ray without ceasing.

1 Thessalonians 5:17

23
Unceasing Intercession

*H*ow different is the standard of the average Christian with regard to a life in the service of God from what Scripture gives us. In the former, the chief thought is personal safety—grace to pardon our sin and to live such a life as may secure our entrance into heaven. How high above this is the Bible standard—a Christian surrendering himself with all his powers, with his time and thought and love wholly yielded to the glorious God who has redeemed him and whom he now delights in serving, in whose fellowship heaven is begun.

To the former, the command "pray without ceasing" is simply a needless and impossible life of perfection: "Who can do it? We can get to heaven without it." To the true believer, on the other hand, it holds out the promise of the highest happiness, of a life crowned by all the blessings that can be brought down on souls around through his intercession. And as he perseveres it becomes increasingly his highest aim upon earth, his highest joy, his highest experience of the wonderful fellowship with the holy God.

"Pray without ceasing!" Let us take that word in a

large faith as a promise of what God's Spirit will work in us, of how close and intimate our union to the Lord Jesus can be, and our likeness to Him, in His ever-blessed intercession at the right hand of God. Let it become to us one of the chief elements of our heavenly calling to be consciously the stewards and administrators of God's grace to the world around us. As we think of how Christ said, "I in them, and thou in me," let us believe that just as the Father worked in Him, so *Christ, the interceding High Priest, will work and pray in us.* As the faith of our high calling fills our hearts, we shall begin literally to feel that there is nothing on earth for one moment to be compared with the privilege of being God's priests, walking without intermission in His holy presence, bringing the burden of the souls around us to the footstool of His throne, and receiving at His hands the power and blessing to dispense to our fellowmen.

This is indeed the fulfillment of the word of old: "Man created in the likeness and the image of God."

The Practice of Intercession

True intercessors will not be turned aside from their pleading. If they meet with rebuffs and no answer seems to come to their supplications, they plead on still. It is a wonderful thing to see a mother pleading with God for her son. She begins pleading for him while he lies in the cradle (or before that). She cries to God for him while he is learning to walk. Her prayers follow him through the devious ways of his youth. And when he goes away from home, and parental restraint is gone; as he roams over the large world, his mother's prayers accompany him. Even though he becomes a Sabbath breaker, a swearer, and says hard things about her church, she persists in praying for him.

She cannot pray, "Lord, save my son, for there is in him some good thing toward you." No, she cries, "Oh, you who are mighty to save, I cannot let you go until you save my poor sinful boy! Have you not said, 'Call upon me in the day of trouble; I will deliver you, and you shall glorify me'? Lord, I am troubled about my son. I beseech you to have pity upon him and save him. Didn't you listen to the Syrophoenician woman when she prayed for her child? Oh, hear me as I pray for mine!"

I hope you know what I mean because you too have prayed for others without ceasing. When you are greatly discouraged, seeing those who are subjects of your prayers going from bad to worse, seeing them more hardened of heart and apparently incorrigible, seeing the seven arrows of the Word of God do not seem to touch them, still persevere in prayer. Yes, until their souls have passed beyond the reach of change, pursue them with your persistent intercession.

*D*ear Father, it is easy for me to pray for members of my family who need to be saved or have other pressing needs met. Help me to love the unlovely sinner, who makes the lives of so many miserable, that I might pray without ceasing for him and see him saved for Jesus' sake. Amen.

*T*hy will be done, as in heaven, so on earth.

Luke 11:2

24
Intercession: The Link Between Heaven and Earth

When God created heaven and earth, He meant heaven to be the divine pattern to which earth was to be conformed: "as in heaven, so on earth" was the law of its existence.

This truth calls us to think of what constitutes the glory of heaven. God is all in all there. Everything lives in Him and to His glory. And as we then think of what this earth has now become, with all its sin and misery, with the great majority of the race without any knowledge of the true God, and the remainder nominally Christians, yet for the greater part utterly indifferent to His claims and estranged from His holiness and love, we feel what a revolution, what a miracle is needed if the word is to be fulfilled: "As in heaven, so on earth."

And how is this ever to come true? *Through the prayers*

of God's children. Our Lord teaches us to pray for it. Intercession is to be the great link between heaven and earth. The intercession of the Son, begun upon earth, continued in heaven, and carried on by His redeemed people upon earth, will bring about the mighty change: "As in heaven, so on earth." As Christ said, "I come to do thy will, O God," until He prayed the great prayer in Gethsemane, "Thy will be done"; so His redeemed ones, who yield themselves fully to His mind and Spirit, make His prayer their own and unceasingly send up the cry, "Thy will be done, as in heaven, so on earth."

Every prayer of a parent for a child, of a believer for the saving of the lost, or for more grace to those who have been saved, is part of the great unceasing cry going up day and night from this earth, "As in heaven, so on earth."

But when God's children not only learn to pray for their immediate circles and interests, but enlarge their hearts to take in the whole Church and the whole world, their united supplication will have power with God and hasten the day when it shall indeed be "as in heaven so on earth"—the whole earth filled with the glory of God. Child of God, will you not yield yourself, like Christ, to live with this one prayer: "Father, Thy will be done on earth as in heaven"?

The Practice of Intercession

Praying in the Spirit gives absolute certainty of success in prayer. If my prayer were my own prayer, I might not be sure of it. But if my prayer is God's own prayer written on my soul, then what He writes on my heart is only written there because it is written in one of His purposes. An old theologian once said that prayer is the shadow of Omnipotence. Our will, when God the Holy Spirit influences it, is the indicator of God's will. When God's people pray, it is because the blessing is coming, and their prayers are the shadow of the coming blessing.

God is neither infirm in memory nor contradictory. What He promised yesterday, He fulfills today. What He said in one place, He declares in another. If God says in my heart, "Pray for So-and-So," it is because He has said it in the book of His decrees. The Spirit of God's writing in the heart always tallies with the writing of destiny in the book of God's eternal purposes.

You cannot help but succeed when you have laid your soul like a sheet of paper before the Lord and asked Him to write upon it. Then it is no more your own prayer merely, but the Spirit making intercession in you according to the will of God. At such time you need not say, "I hope God will answer my prayer." He will do it—He has pledged to do it.

Oh! If more of you tried Him as some of us have been compelled to do, you would have to hold up your hands in astonishment, and say, "Verily, whatever else is not a fact, it *is* a fact that God who sits in the highest heavens listens to the cries of His people and gives them the desires of their hearts."

*D*ear Holy Spirit, thank you for teaching me how to pray. I will take time today to get quiet before you and have you write the will of God upon my soul for myself and others that I might pray rightly in faith. Amen.

The Lord hath desired
Zion for his habitation.
Here will I dwell; for I have
desired it.

Psalm 132:13, 14

25
The Fulfillment of God's Desires

*I*n this verse you have the one great desire of God that moved Him in the work of redemption: His heart longed for man—to dwell with him and in him.

To Moses He said: "Let them make me a sanctuary; that I may dwell among them." And just as Israel had to prepare the dwelling for God, even so His children are now called to yield themselves for God to dwell in them, and to win others to become His habitation. As the desire of God toward us fills the heart, it will waken within us the desire to gather others around us to become His dwelling too.

What an honor! What a high calling to count my worldly business as entirely secondary and to find my life and my delight in winning souls in whom God may find His heart's delight! "Here will I dwell; for I have desired it."

And this is what I can above all do through intercession. I can pray for God to give His Holy Spirit to those around me. It is God's great plan that man himself shall build Him a habitation. In answer to the unceasing intercession of His children God will give His power and blessing. As this great desire of God fills us, we shall give ourselves wholly to labor for its fulfillment.

Think of David when he thought of God's desire to dwell in Israel; he said: "I will not give sleep to my eyes, nor slumber to mine eyelids, until I find a place for the Lord, an habitation for the mighty God of Jacob." And shall not those of us who know what that indwelling of God may be give our lives for the fulfillment of His heart's desire?

Oh, let us begin, as never before, to pray for our children, for the souls around us, and for all the world. Let us pray not only because we love them, but because God longs for them and gives us the honor of being the channels through whom His blessing is brought down. Children of God, awake to the realization of what it means that God is seeking to train you as intercessors, through whom the great desire of His loving heart can be satisfied!

The Practice of Intercession

The most essential thing you can do for the conversion of sinners is pray. What can you do by yourself in converting anyone? You cannot change his heart. You cannot put life into him: you might as well think you can create a soul within the ribs of death. God regenerates souls. You are to be an instrument in conversion, and your very first action must be to fall on your knees and pray, "O God, work in me and with me."

Perhaps you will be going to church today to preach or teach, or perhaps you are going out to witness in the streets. Now, if *you* could do the work by yourself, I would not urge you to waste any time in asking God to do what you could do alone. But since you are utterly powerless to win a single soul to Jesus without the Spirit of God within you and working with you, let your very first action be to pray, "O power divine, come and clothe me! O tongue of fire, be given to me. Sacred, rushing, mighty wind, come forth to breathe life upon dead souls!" Prayer is the most essential thing in turning sinners from the error of their ways.

Intercessory prayer will fit you to become God's instrument. If I pray for a person's conversion, especially if I single out some particular individual, then as I think over his position and condition in prayer, my heart gets warmed into love for that person. Prayer instructs me and helps me to give the proper word to him. I am like a surgeon who knows the correct diagnosis and how to operate; this is given to me by prayer. When I have considered my petitions, I know practically how to work upon the sinner, and I shall be wise in the Spirit of God to do the right thing in the right way. Intercession is the way to become wise in winning souls.

Come, Holy Spirit. Come as a burning fire and purify my motives. Cleanse me from all unrighteousness. Fit me for the conversion of others. Whenever I am with any sinner I have been praying for teach me what to say and when to say it, that your desires might be fulfilled. Amen.

Delight thyself in the Lord, and he shall give thee the desires of thine heart.

Psalm 37:4

26

The Fulfillment of Man's Desires

God is love. God is an ever-flowing fountain, out of whom streams an unceasing desire to make His creatures the partakers of all the holiness and blessedness there is in himself. This desire for the salvation of souls is indeed God's perfect will, His highest glory.

God's loving desire is to take His place in the heart of people. He imparts himself to those who yield themselves wholly to Him. Having the likeness and image of God in us means to have a heart in which His love takes complete possession, leading us to find spontaneously our highest joy in loving as He loves. Thus our text finds its fulfillment: "Delight thyself in the Lord," and in His life of love, "he will give thee the desires of thine heart." Count upon it: the intercession of love, rising up to heaven, will be met with the fulfillment of the desires of our hearts. We may be sure that, as we delight in what God delights in, such prayer is inspired by God and will have its answer. And our prayer becomes unceasingly, "Thy desires, O my Father, are mine. Thy holy will of love is my will too."

In fellowship with Him, we get the courage with our whole will and strength to bring before His throne the people or the circles in which we are interested, with an ever-growing confidence that our prayer will be heard. As we reach out in yearning love, we shall get the power to take hold of the will of God to bless, and to believe that God will work out His own blessed will in giving us the desire of our hearts—because the fulfillment of His desire has been the delight of our souls.

In the highest sense of the word, we then become God's fellow-laborers. Our prayer becomes part of God's divine work of reaching and saving the lost. And we learn to find our happiness in losing ourselves in the salvation of those around us.

The Practice of Intercession

Prayer *in the Holy Spirit* is indispensable. The phrase means, first, praying in the Holy Spirit's *power*. The carnal mind knows nothing about this. I might as well talk in high Dutch as in English upon this point to an unregenerate man. But regenerate men, people who are born of the Spirit and live in the Spirit world, are aware of communications between their spirits and the Holy Spirit who resides in the midst of the Church of God.

We know that the Divine Spirit, without the use of sounds, speaks in our hearts. He can make our souls know His presence and understand His meaning. He casts the spiritual shadow of His influence over us, coloring our thoughts and feelings according to His own design and will.

This is a great spiritual fact: the Christian knows for certain that the Holy Spirit, the Divine Spirit, has frequent dealings with spiritual minds and imparts to them His power. Our newborn spirit has a certain degree of power, but the power is never fully manifested or drawn out unless the Spirit of God quickens our spirit and excites us to activity. Our spirit prays when it is overshadowed and filled with the power of the Holy Spirit.

If I went to the throne of grace and only prayed as my fleshly nature prayed, my prayer would not be acceptable. When I go to the mercy seat and my new nature prays as the Holy Spirit enables me to pray, then my prayer will succeed with God.

If I come before God and His eternal Spirit speaks to my soul and lifts it out of the dead level of fallen humanity and brings it up to be filled with divine force; if the Spirit is in me as a well of water springing up unto everlasting life; if I receive the divine light and power of the Holy Spirit, and if in His power I fervently draw near to God, my prayer will prevail with God. This power may be possessed by every Christian.

*D*ear Father, you do not desire that any should perish. You desire that all should come to repentance and faith. Help me to pray unceasingly for some who seem to be hopeless cases, for some who rebuke me for my evangelical faith. Save them so they can be of great use to you. Amen.

*One thing have I desired
of the Lord, that will I seek
after: that I may dwell in
the house of the Lord all the
days of my life, to behold the
beauty of the Lord, and to
inquire in his temple.*

Psalm 27:4

27
My Great Desire

Here we have our response to God's desire to dwell in us. When the desire of God toward us begins to rule our life and heart, our desire is fixed on one thing: to dwell in the house of the Lord all the days of our life, to behold the beauty of the Lord, to worship Him in the beauty of holiness. And then to inquire in His temple and learn what it means for Him to say: "I the Lord have spoken it, and will do it. And I will yet for this be inquired of by the house of Israel to do it for them."

We must realize that the desire of God's love is to give His rest in our hearts. The more our desire is thus quickened to dwell every day in His temple and behold His beauty, the more the Spirit of intercession will grow upon us to claim all that God has promised in His new covenant. Whether we think of our church and country, of our home and school, of our nearer or wider circle; whether we think of the saved and all their needs or the unsaved and their danger, the thought that God is indeed longing to find His home and His rest in the hearts of people, if only He is *inquired of*, will rouse our whole being to strive for the

Church's sake not to hold our peace. All the thoughts of our feebleness and unworthiness will be swallowed up in the wonderful assurance that He has said of human hearts: "This is my rest for ever; here will I dwell, for I have desired it."

As our faith sees how high our calling is, how indispensable God has made fervent, intense, persistent prayer as the condition of His purpose being fulfilled, we shall be drawn to give up our life to a closer walk with God, to an unceasing waiting upon Him, and to a testimony to our brothers and sisters in Christ of what God will do in them and in us.

Is it not wonderful beyond all thought, this divine partnership in which God commits the fulfillment of His desires to our keeping? Shame upon us that we have so little realized it!

The Practice of Intercession

Praying in the Holy Spirit is surely praying in a *holy* frame of mind. Do you ever get distracted in your mind as you are praying? Some of you leave your homes for worship, saying, "This is the blessed Sabbath, and I feel I have God's presence." But then you come into worship feeling burdened because you met some silly gossip on the steps of the church. Some idle tale has distracted you. Or, you get quietly seated and then remember something someone said six weeks earlier, and your mind is perplexed and you cannot pray. But when the Holy Spirit comes, He will take a scourge of small cords and drive these buyers and sellers out of the temple of your mind and leave it clear for God. Then you can come to God with a holy, devout frame of mind, fixed and settled in your great object of worship of God. This is to approach Him in the Holy

Spirit. Pray for the Holy Spirit to drive any unwelcome thoughts and desires out of your mind before you approach God in worship or prayer. Oh, for more of this blessed, undisturbed devotion!

Praying in the Holy Spirit means praying *humbly* and recognizing your dependence on Him. The Holy Spirit never puffs up anyone with pride. He is the Spirit that convinces of sin, and so bows us down with a broken and contrite spirit. We must pray to God as the humble publican, or we shall never come from worship justified as he was.

*D*ear Heavenly Father, the only rest I can have in my mind is the rest you give by your presence. So fill my mind with your precious, loving Spirit until there remains no room for unholy or unwelcome distractions when I pray. Fill my mind with the thoughts you want me to have, with the people you want me to intercede for, with the causes you hold most dear to your heart. Bring these thoughts before me one at a time, focus my attention upon them for as long as needed to achieve your purpose. Help me as I intercede in your glorious light for your glorious purpose. Amen.

*S*hall not God avenge his
own elect, which cry day
and night unto him, though
he bear long with them?

Luke 18:7

28

Intercession Day and Night

When Nehemiah heard of the destruction of Jerusalem, he cried to God: "Hear the prayer of thy servant which I pray before thy face day and night." Of the watchmen set on the walls of Jerusalem, God said: "Who shall never hold their peace day nor night." And Paul wrote: "Night and day praying exceedingly, to the end he may establish your hearts unblameable in holiness before our God and Father."

Is such prayer night and day really needed and really possible? Most assuredly, when the heart is first so entirely possessed by the desire that it cannot rest until it is fulfilled. It is possible when the life has so come under the power of the heavenly blessing that nothing can keep it from sacrificing all to obtain it.

When a child of God begins to get a real vision into the need of the Church and of the world, a vision of the divine redemption that God has promised in the outpouring of His love into our hearts, a vision of the power of true intercession to bring down the heavenly blessing, a vision of the honor of being allowed as intercessors to take part in that work, it comes as a matter of course that He regards the work as the most heavenly thing upon earth—as intercessor to cry day and night to God for the revelation of His mighty power.

Let us learn from David, who said: "The zeal of thine house hath consumed me." From Christ our Lord, of whom these words were so intensely true, let us learn that there is nothing so much worth living for as this one thought—how to satisfy the heart of God in His longing for human fellowship and affection, and how to win hearts to be His dwelling-place. And shall not we, too, give ourselves no rest until we have found a place for the Mighty One in our hearts, and yielded ourselves to the great work of intercession for so many after whom the desires of God are going out?

God grant that our hearts may be so brought under the influence of these divine truths that we may in very deed yield ourselves to make our devotion to Christ and our longing to satisfy the heart of God the chief object of our life.

The Practice of Intercession

The carnal man, if he is foolish enough, can intone a prayer. The carnal man can "do his duty" as well as anyone who can read a prayer book. But he is not praying. Only the spiritual man can sigh and long, cry in his inmost heart and in the chamber of his soul before God, and he will not do it unless the Spirit of truth leads him in sincerity into the secret of heart-prayer.

Praying in the Holy Spirit is praying in *fervency*. Cold prayers are like asking God *not* to hear them. Those who do not plead with fervency do not plead at all. You may as well speak of lukewarm fire as of lukewarm prayer. True prayer is red hot. Real prayer is burned like hot iron into a person's soul, and then comes forth from his soul like coals of juniper, which have the most awesome heat. Such prayers no one but the Holy Spirit can give.

A few months ago there were times when some of our brothers were helped to pray with such power that we were bowed down in humiliation, and then we were lifted up as on the wings of eagles in the power of supplication. There is a way of praying with power in which a person seems to get hold of the posts of heaven's gate, as Samson grasped the pillars of the temple, and appears as though he would pull all down upon himself sooner than miss the blessing.

It is a brave thing for anyone to vow, "I will not let thee go except thou bless me." That is praying in the Holy Spirit. May He teach us the art of offering effectual fervent prayer!

*D*ear Holy Spirit, I long for a closeness with you that words cannot describe. I long to pray effectively, so I can bless others. I long to see your vision for my life, so I can pray specifically for that vision to be fulfilled. Teach me to pray in faith until the blessing comes. Amen.

We have such an high priest . . . who is able to save them to the uttermost that come unto God by him, seeing he ever liveth to make intercession for them.

Hebrews 8:1a, 7:25

29
The High Priest and His Intercession

*I*n Israel what a difference there was between the high priest and the priests and the Levites. The high priest alone had access to the Holiest of All. He bore on his forehead the golden crown, engraved with "Holiness to the Lord," and by his intercession on the great Day of Atonement bore the sins of the people. The priests brought the daily sacrifices and stood before the Lord, then came out to bless the people. The difference between high priest and priest was great. But still greater was the unity. They formed one body with the high priest, sharing with him the power to appear before God to receive and dispense His blessing to His people.

It is even so with our great High Priest. He alone has power with God in a never-ceasing intercession to obtain from the Father what His people need. And yet, infinite though the distance is between Him and the royal priesthood that surrounds Him for His service, the unity and the fellowship into which His people have been taken up with

Him is no less infinite than the apparent diversity. The blessing that He obtains from His Father, He gives to His people through their fervent prayers to dispense to the souls among whom they have been placed as His witnesses and representatives.

As long as Christians simply think of being saved, and of a life which will make that salvation secure, they never can understand the mystery of the power of intercession to which they are called. But when once they realize that salvation means a vital life-union with Jesus Christ, an actual sharing of His life dwelling and working in them, and the consecration of their whole being to live and labor, to think and will, and find their highest joy in living as a royal priesthood, the Church will put on her strength and prove how truly the likeness and the power of Christ dwells in her.

The Practice of Intercession

True prayer must be loving prayer if it is praying in the Holy Spirit. Prayer must be perfumed with love, saturated with love, love to Christ and your fellow saints.

True prayer must be full of faith. The effectual fervent prayer of a person prevails only as he believes in God; and the Holy Spirit is the author of faith in us. The Holy Spirit nurtures and strengthens our faith so that we can pray believing God's promises.

If you have ever felt His love shed abroad in your heart, if you have been washed in His blood, if you have been saved from wrath through Him, if you are a new creature in Him, if you hope to see His face with acceptance at last, then pray in the Holy Spirit.

If you refuse to unite with your brothers and sisters in prayer, if you refuse to pray in the Holy Spirit now that He has been given, if you refuse now to go before your great High Priest, then you may feel yourself deprived of the comfortable presence of the Holy Spirit and find the sweetness of devotion departed from you.

You must approach God believing that He will send His blessing in answer to prayer. You must approach Him feeling that your heart will break if He does not hear you. Grasp His promises. Plead with God. Continue to plead with God until His blessing comes. Plead the blood of Jesus. He is even now your High Priest in heaven. Rely upon it: the heavenly shower will descend. Be hopeful. Unite in prayer with your brothers and sisters in Christ. Unanimously pray in the Holy Spirit. Pray in Jesus' name and for His sake.

Remember, God ever hears our prayers according to our inward groaning. He notices the longing, the desiring, the sighing, the crying. Your outward prayer is but the shell, your inward prayer is the true kernel and essence.

Dear Father, often I cannot express in words the gnawing anxiety I sometimes feel. I cannot put my finger on the cause of my inner distress. So I pray that you who know my heart will give me peace in Jesus. Amen.

*Call unto me, and I will
answer thee, and show thee
great and mighty things,
which thou knowest not.*

Jeremiah 33:3

30
A Royal Priesthood

*A*s you plead for the great mercies of the new covenant to be bestowed, remember the infinite willingness of God to bless. His very nature is a pledge of it. He delights in mercy. He waits to be gracious. His promises and the experience of His saints assure us of it.

Why, then, does the blessing so often tarry? In creating you with a free will and making you a partner in the rule of the earth, God limited himself. He made himself dependent on what you would do. You, by your prayer, hold the measure of what God will do in blessing.

Think of how God is hindered and disappointed when His children do not pray or pray very little. The low, feeble life of the Church, the lack of the power of the Holy Spirit for conversion and holiness, is all due to the lack of prayer. How different the state of the Church and world would be if God's people would take no rest in calling upon Him!

God has blessed according to the measure of the faith and the zeal of His people. They must not be content with this as a sign of His approval, but rather say, "If He has thus blessed our feeble efforts and prayers, what will He not do if we yield ourselves wholly to a life of intercession?"

What a call to repentance and confession! Our lack of consecration has kept back God's blessing from the world! He was ready to save people, but we were not willing to make the sacrifice of a wholehearted devotion to Christ and His service.

Children of God, God counts upon you to take your place before His throne as intercessors. Awake, I pray you, to the consciousness of your holy calling as a royal priesthood. Begin to live a new life in the assurance that intercession, in both the likeness to and the fellowship with the interceding Lord Jesus in heaven, is the highest privilege a person can desire. In this spirit take up the word with large expectations: "Call unto me, and I will answer thee, and show thee great and mighty things which thou knowest not."

Are you willing to give yourself wholly to this blessed calling? In the power of Jesus Christ, are you willing to make the one chief object of your life intercession and supplication for God's Church and people and for a dying world? Is this asking too much of you? Is it too much to ask you to yield your life for this holy service of the royal priesthood?

The Practice of Intercession

The prayer meeting is the place for the reception of divine power. What a difference the disciples' first prayer meeting made in them! Common fishermen became the extraordinary messengers of heaven. Illiterate men spoke with tongues they had never heard before. They began to reveal mysteries of God that had not been revealed by philosophers or kings. These men were lifted out of the level of ordinary humanity and became God-inspired, filled with the Deity, who came to dwell in their hearts and minds. As the result of prayer, poor, wavering Peter became bold as a lion, and impetuous John (who would have called down fire from heaven upon the Samaritans) had another fire fall upon him—one to rescue and bless instead of destroy.

The great lack of the Church today is the power of the Holy Spirit. The Apostles' Creed says: "I believe in the Holy Ghost," but how many are there who really do believe in Him? The Third Person of the blessed Trinity will still give us spiritual power today. If we would have the Holy Spirit, we must pray with greater fervency, earnestness and steadfastness, and we must pray in greater numbers in the Church.

Dear Father, keep me from being so concerned about the proper form of my prayers that I fail to see prayer as a supernatural personal relationship with you which allows me to speak to you in behalf of myself and many others. I praise you for making this possible through Christ and enabling me to pray in fellowship with Him today. Amen.

*A*nd another angel came
. . . and there was given
unto him much incense, that
he should offer it with the
prayers of all saints upon the
golden altar which was
before the throne.

Revelation 8:3

31

Intercession: A Divine Reality

*A*re the thoughts of this little book a sufficiently grave indictment of the subordinate place given to intercession in the Church? Is it not of such supreme importance as to make it an essential, altogether indispensable element in the true Christian life? To those who take God's Word in its full meaning, there can be no doubt about the answer.

Intercession is by amazing grace an essential element in God's redeeming purpose—so much so that without it the failure of its accomplishment may lie at our door. Christ's intercession in heaven is essential to His carrying out of the work He began upon earth, but He calls for the intercession of the saints in the attainment of His object. Just think of what we read: "All things are of God, who hath reconciled us to himself by Jesus Christ, and hath given to us the ministry of reconciliation." As the reconciliation was dependent on Christ's doing His part, so in the accomplishment of the work He calls on the Church to do her part. Paul regarded intercession day and night as indispensable to the fulfillment of the work that had been entrusted to him. It is but one aspect of that mighty power of God which works in the heart of His believing people.

Intercession is indeed a divine reality. Without it the Church loses one of its chief beauties, loses the joy and the power of the Spirit life for achieving great things for God. Without it, there is no power for the Church to recover from her sickly, feeble life and conquer the world. And in the life of the believer, minister or member, there can be no entrance into the abundant life and joy of daily fellowship with God, except as he takes his place among God's elect—the watchmen and remembrancers of God, who cry to Him day and night.

Church of Christ, awake, awake! Listen to the call: "Pray without ceasing. Take no rest, and give God no rest." Let the answer be, even though it be with a sigh from the depths of the heart: "For Zion's sake will I not hold my peace." God's Spirit will reveal to us the power of a life of intercession as a divine reality, an essential and indispensable element of the great redemption, and therefore also of the true Christian life. May God help us to know and fulfill our calling!

The Practice of Intercession

God has promised extraordinary and peculiar blessings in connection with united intercessory prayer: "If two of you shall agree on earth as touching anything that they shall ask, it shall be done for them of my Father which is in heaven." God asks agreement, and once the saints agree, He pledges himself that their prayer will be answered. See what accumulated force there is in this type of prayer. When one after another pours out his intense desires, when many seem to be tugging at the rope, when many seem to be knocking at mercy's gate, when the mighty cries of many burning hearts come up to heaven, when you go and shake the very gates with the powerful battering ram of earnest and sacred prayers, then God answers.

Think of the accumulated love of God there is in a prayer meeting, because God loves each of His children. There is so much love for one and then another and another, and so much love for God, that surely there must be a force of love to move our heavenly Father to grant the accumulated desires of His people.

Lift up your heart to God in real prayer. He has given us His pledge that He will answer. Believe it and you shall see it, and you shall have the joy of it while He shall have the glory.

*D*ear Father, if I compare my efforts at intercession with the teachings in this book, I am humbled and convicted of my lack of fervent, persevering prayer. Grant me strength as I resolve to spend more time in prayer than I spend in the daily study of how to pray. In Jesus' name. Amen.